A Spiritual Traveler's Guide
To Sacred Mount Shasta
Prophecy
2014-2020

Susan Isabelle

Susan Isabelle

ISBN-13: 978-1494853822

ISBN-10: 1494853825

DEDICATION

This book is dedicated to all those that are seeking the Higher Path to Enlightenment, to those that are serious about their spiritual wellbeing and that of this planet!

Blessings!

CONTENTS

ACKNOWLEDGMENTS

I am grateful to those that help to make Mount Shasta a beautiful home and a vast, diverse spiritual community.

To Karuk Elder Charlie Red Hawk Thom 4/4/1928-10/08/2013

To Forestry and National Parks personnel that help us to preserve and protect this vast, spiritual mountain.

To the Native American Tribal efforts to keep this land sacred.

I acknowledge your work and thank you for all that you do.

A special thanks to my partner, Jeremiah, for his patience and loving support, vast knowledge, assistance and compassion.

i

CHAPTER 1 A WORD TO SPIRITUAL TRAVELERS

Yreka, Ca. Route I-5 South, 25 miles north of Mt Shasta

Every year I have the opportunity to meet and to enjoy the presence of wonderful seekers of enlightenment. Daily, spiritual seekers arrive at Mount Shasta, California and the little City of Mt. Shasta may see many thousands of visitors arrive each year.

They come from all across the globe; China, Japan, Australia, Italy, Spain, Argentina, Mexico and so many more countries. I have seen people from thirty three countries come here so far.

Why? Each, in their own way, has come to receive a blessing, a vision, enlightenment, hope, and to pray.

Why Mount Shasta?

She is the one of the most sacred places on planet Earth.

Mount Shasta & Shastina

In 1999 I came here on a spiritual quest, just as many of you have, because of the 'Call' of Mount Shasta. Once I arrived I had many adventures on the mountain. Afterward, I would never be the same. While you are here, I'd like you to have this experience too!

I moved to Mt. Shasta from New Hampshire in 2004. I now own and operate the Shambhala Ministries and Store in the center of the City of Mt. Shasta. It gives me an opportunity to share with many people each year the wonders of this very sacred mountain as they eventually make their way into my store. I know that every day is a new day in Mt Shasta, and brings with it an opportunity to expand one's consciousness and grow to new spiritual heights. But, one must desire it.

When I first arrived here in 1999, I wish I'd have had a guidebook to help me understand what was happening to me! So I write to you of some of my experiences and adventures over the past ten years in Shasta. There have been many! In this book I bring you sacred knowledge secured within the stories.

I will speak to you of the wondrous spiritual sites at Shasta, especially Kuan Yin's Temple. I located her temple the first summer that I moved here. I think that everyone ought make the pilgrimage to go there. She will bless your soul with peace.

I will speak to you extensively of the local Native American beliefs and how to honor their presence here also. It is my hope that you will have a higher spiritual experience while at this sacred mountain by following some simple instructions.

Yes, UFO's, and Bigfoot are also part of my experience too! In my stories about them you will find the way to establish a connection, what to do when you make contact, and how you may also attain the gifting. This privilege of having the connection has some requirements fulfilled beforehand.

I have included a special meditation to assist the reader to reconnect back to the Divine Template, to restore the true essence of your own being;

Shasta will accept nothing else!

You will learn the first things to do when you arrive to properly prepare yourself. I have sought to give you solid advice through my personal experiences, mistakes, and example.

I will also bring to you PROPHECY 2020

At the end of this writing, I will attempt to explain what I believe are events that will be coming on the earth between the dates of April 2014 and that of 2020. I will also attempt to explain my reasons for believing what I do.

Some of you will be surprised because of a preconception of my being totally 'metaphysical.' I am after all the Keeper of the 13th Crystal Skull of the Maya.

My beliefs in the end times prophecies of the Creator of All and the Holy Scriptures run very deep. It is my understanding of deep mysteries of scripture, of the Maya, Kabbala, Native American and many other cultures that have given me insight and Divine guidance.

That is really how I became Keeper of the 13th Skull. People are always asking me why I was 'chosen' to receive the skull. I feel the envy, it hurts, and I receive letters from people that are angry as well as those who understand its' cost to my life.

All I can say is that Spirit has guided my every step to find understanding and to have an open mind to receive that guidance. Then, I did what needed to be done, sometimes even at the risk of my own life.

I have given all of my life to being a Spiritual Traveler on Earth seeking to do the will of the Creator Of All and to fulfill the prophecies and assignments that have been given to me to do. I will explain more in the final chapters.

I have written this book to assist you, the Spiritual Traveler, to attain deep Spiritual knowledge, to understand the processes required to actualize one's personal goals, and to find what your soul is truly seeking while at Mount Shasta.

The True Spiritual Seeker will not be disappointed! The stories are true, are instructional in themselves, and are real page turners!

But before we delve into the spiritual aspects of Mount Shasta and how you may attain a higher level of enlightenment from this sacred mountain, let us first establish some facts.

Weed, Ca.

Chapter 2
MOUNTAIN FACTS

The mountain stands nearly 10,000 ft. above the surrounding landscape. Her actual elevation is 14,179 feet. As you travel around the mountain, it may seem that you are viewing several different mountains! All one, but each facet of the mountain viewed from another direction brings mystery and a beauty to the soul of the beholder. On a clear winter day snowy Mount Shasta can be seen as far away as 140 miles from the south.

Mount Shasta has four overlapping volcanic cones that form its shape, the main summit is Mt Shasta at 14,179 feet and the prominent Shastina, called a satellite cone, stands beside Mount Shasta at 12,330 feet.

There are seven glaciers on Mount Shasta, the four largest are Whitney, Bolam, Hotlum and Wintun.

7

Abram's Lake Exit

The Native American Presence

One cannot enter onto sacred ground or seek a spiritual experience while ignoring the obvious; this is sacred Native American ground. The Native peoples have much to say as they have been here for a long, long time. This mountain is sacred to many of the tribes surrounding Mount Shasta, even though they may have different views and legends. They must be heard.

Their customs and religious beliefs predate any thoughts the incoming settlers may have had, or any subsequent newer age teachings. We need to listen to their wisdom to begin to understand this mountain. We will spend time to discover some of the ancient, sacred ways of the people who live here.

The Klamath Tribe, the Wintu, Modoc, Pit River Tribes, the Karuk and Shasta Indians, all view the sacredness of the mountain with great awe. The tribes continue to hold Native American ceremonies and rituals at the mountain as they have done so for thousands of years. It is logical that we seek this wisdom for understanding and our personal growth.

The Klamath Tribal legends state that Mount Shasta is inhabited by the Spirit of the Above-World, Skell. It is told that He descended from heaven to the mountain's summit at the request of a Klamath chief.

Skell fought with Spirit of the Below-World called Llao, who had resided at Mount Mazama, now known as Crater Lake in Oregon. It was destroyed in the battle, the volcano collapsed and the resulting caldera has become known as Crater Lake. Good overcomes darkness at Shasta! Strong, righteous energies are here!

Counting the Prayer Ties

A custom of the Native peoples is to place tobacco and other sacred herbs in little tied colored cloth packets while saying a prayer into each one as a blessing, for ceremony and gifts.

The Shasta & Pit River Tribal Legends

Places such as Mt. Shasta continue to be important spiritually to the Shasta. For example, the Shasta have recently stated that the area above tree line on Mt. Shasta is sacred to them, and only the dead go there. You will see this demonstrated later in this writing through my own experience. Resource; Draft Environmental Impact Statement, Mt. Shasta Wilderness Plan, p. 111?33.

Like the Shasta, Pit River or Achumawi myths often involve creatures of some kind. For instance, in "the Fury of Loon Woman," Loon Woman, in a fit of revenge, burns several creatures such as Coyote, Wildcat, Lizard, etc. As they burn in the fire, their hearts pop out and are caught by Loon Woman in a basket. *One heart escaped and landed on Mount Shasta*! Perhaps that legend is why people find hearts up there all the time ! You may also find a little heart shaped stone on your journey. Resource ; http://www.siskiyous.edu/shasta/fol/nat/henn.htm

Sweat Lodge Ceremonies

Sweat Lodge ceremonies are held all around Mount Shasta by Native and non-native peoples. Stewart Mineral Springs in Weed, Ca. hosts a public sweat lodge on Saturdays. http://www.stewartmineralsprings.com/nodes/events/sweatlodge.htm

You may want to attend as this is a beautiful lodge held by Karuk Elder Charlie Thom's nephew, Jack Thom. Jack is Sundance Leader, a healer and counselor. He has carried on Charlie's work, and has made this lodge available to you.

Later on in this book, you will learn about the importance of honoring your Elders, and to the benefit to your own soul, of proper return payment. This is wise. When you arrive at the sweat lodge, no one will ask you for money, but there is a donation box that is used to help pay for the lodge costs, the wood, and assist the Elder. Please be generous! If you needed healing spiritually or physically, what would you pay your doctor? This is your opportunity to receive a blessing!

Mount Shasta also hosts more private Lodge ceremonies and you may be invited. If you have never been to a sweat lodge here are a few tips;

Sweat Lodge Tips

Understand that a sweat lodge is someone's Church, not a curiosity. Please dress modestly and women on their 'moon time,' period, should not enter the Lodge to avoid complications or later   having to be assisted out. A special feminine lodge is also available for you during your moon cycle.

When you enter a sweat lodge know that the Elder is just that. Honor and respect the Elder for his knowledge and dedication to Mother Earth, Creator and this kindness that is being extended to you.

The fire pit is sacred; please, don't throw anything into it. The area between the fire pit and the front of the Lodge is not to be crossed or are there to be children running back and forth.

Follow the lead of the Elders, they will help you by their leading; they do not tell you what to do, so follow. Smudging is done outside the Lodge prior to entering to cleanse your aura.

As you enter the Lodge remember, it is a Church. Alcohol

and drugs are not allow. Be clean before you enter a Lodge.

No jewelry, cameras, water bottles, shoes etc: are allowed inside. You may want to have a towel to sit upon or to use over your head during parts of the ceremony. Bring water to drink in between rounds and to cool off.

Touch the Sacred Earth of the Lodge as you are entering into the Womb of Mother. Honor your Mother and what is about to happen. You are reborn, cleansed in Her Womb.

Turn to the left and find a place that you may sit. If it is your first time in a Lodge, know that it gets quite warm in there, so a place to the sides of the Lodge will afford you some protection from the heat of the rocks brought in from the fire pit. Do not attempt to put anything on or near the rocks. The rocks from the fire pit are *very* hot; they are the Rock Nation. They are honored, brushed off and are made ready to receive the medicines placed on them during the Lodge ceremony that *only* the Elder or designee may place on the rocks.

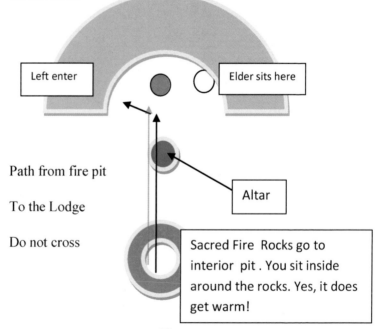

Left enter

Elder sits here

Path from fire pit

To the Lodge

Do not cross

Altar

Sacred Fire Rocks go to interior pit . You sit inside around the rocks. Yes, it does get warm!

The water to be used on the rocks is also sacred and honored. It will be placed upon the rocks to create steam that is very cleansing to the mind, body and soul.

The steam lifts our prayers to the Creator. Herbs are used during the ceremony. *You are not allowed to put anything on the rocks.* The Elder does so as he is guided and special herbs are used for healing, for prayers, or cleansing purposes.

There are usually four "doors" or rounds to a sweat lodge ceremony. Each is directed by the Elder. Prayers to Father and Mother Earth are sung and prayed.

In the very unlikely event that you become ill, state *"DOOR!"* and they will allow you to leave. Stay if you reasonably can as many things are released never to return again in the healing that results. Focus your thoughts.

If very hot, place the towel over your head and lie close to Mother earth where it is cooler.

When leaving the Lodge at the end, everyone exits clockwise but not until after the Elder has left the Lodge.

Please enjoy your sacred experience. You may want to go for a refreshing dip in the springs and have a clean change of clothes for afterwards!

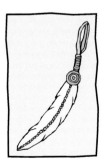

I have a copy of the 20th anniversary edition of Charlie Red Hawk Thom's celebration at Panther Meadow from 2005. Included is a copy of a 1995's newsletter called, *Medicine Song*, I quote Charlie, a prophecy from him, and something that is so frighteningly true nearly 20 years later. He says,

> *"Things that our old people said are coming true. I strongly believe in our Indian Prophecies. I have faith in our old Indian people and their ways. Some things that were said were hard to swallow and believe. We, the Indian people, have been praying sun up to sun down; we see much destruction of Mother Earth, the environment and our sacred places. The time has come to get the message out to everyone on Mother Earth and the world. Start working together; one way to start is with prayer, a very spiritual way."*

Charlie, I still believe we can change things. One of his favorite sayings was that "**we need to walk backwards into the future**." We all need to learn to rediscover the ancient ways and live in harmony with nature once again.

As we look upon Mount Shasta this year and see the snows diminishing with our global warming or climate changes, (no matter what the reason), I quote from his letter once again. Remember, this was 20 years ago;

> *"Our Indian people get very worried when Mount Shasta has very little snow on it. Since the creation we have been taught the mountain must have snow on it at all times or it will be a very bad time-it must have a white cap year round. Many Indian people feel that the mountain will take care of itself, which is possibly true.*
>
> *This day and age, we feel there are lots of crazy people in this world, full of impurities like drugs, alcohol and nicotine, poisoning the body making you feel like you are making the right decision on many issues for the people of this world, when actually you are being guided by the*

impurities in your body and not listening to the real you and helping our Mother Earth.

When the pioneers arrived in Northern California, they destroyed everything they touched. The Shasta and Modec tribes were nearly wiped out. Large bands of Indian people were destroyed by these pioneers.

The Shasta and the Modec tribes did not have the protection the Karuk people did. The Karuk had the mountainous areas of the Klamath and Salmon Rivers to protect them. With the arrival of the pioneers the precious ores gold, silver, copper and other rich minerals were depleted from out sacred land."

Note; I asked Charlie about the gold one afternoon. He explained that the gold had nothing to do with money to the Indians, but it had everything to do with ecology.

Charlie explained to me that when the pioneers filled with greed, took the gold, they removed the metals that prevented the lightning strikes that are now causing the fires across California.

He said that the gold in California held a polarity that dispersed the build up of the electro-magnetic earth forces. He said that this is why we would continue to have weather changes across the earth. As he said, it was the beginning of his people's prophecy and ' hard to swallow.' We are reaping that consequence of taking what was not ours to take, now globally.

Charlie also explained that people were losing their minds from stress of modern living and through impurities. He believed they were incapable of making sound judgments.

Continued;

"Tons of gold that were taken from the land cannot be put back. Our wildlife stock became depleted. The Elk was

15

listed on the endangered species list. It makes me feel good that in the last ten years I have had the pleasure of watching the Elk herd grow in Northern California under the protection of the State and our tribal government.

The sacred white buffalo and the sacred white deer(he saw it 10/24/1994) tell us that our spiritual and cultural ways are coming back strong to the Indian people. We are the leaders of our Mother Earth, we have been selected to put this world back on the right track.

Your support is needed out there, you must remember that I Charlie Red Hawk Thom am just one person, I need your support on many issues, but first you must be healed first and put in physical and spiritual shape.

From there your spirit will guide you to do whatever is needed to help and put this country and the world back on the right track. The Great Spirit has a message to go out to all people. I will be out there doing what the Great Spirit has guided me to do. I work for Ikxareeyav 24 hours a day."

Yootva , Charlie Red Hawk Thom.

I have had the unique opportunity to interview Charlie on many occasions privately. I received a signed permission from Charlie in 2005 to release his stories to the world at the proper time. Even from the other side Charlie's words and wisdom continue to serve Creator. It is time.

I am also of Native lineage, the Iroquois Nation. I hear his words today and also hold the responsibility to get this message out to the world.

I N D I A N,   Same Spirit, Different Life

I   In the spirit world there are echos resounding a light that calls with their every name listed in its' archives. There is a silence heard also that plays the heartstrings' song. To be mindful of the singing ring of the kings' buzz that comes and goes as it will, within the existing realm of your mindfulness. In this there is no wrong.

N ative American Medicine People, hear their voices across the ages still chanting, praying in sons and daughters that beat the drum and sweat the truth. We are those of whom traverse the ageless universe of infinite creation to see the truth lives on. We are the ones that come humbly together, into this our prayer booth.

D ying to the world we come from in the melding mix of socially impacted domestic rules and governings, we decide our spirit shall live this the old way. For what we pray is what we mean in everything we live and do in our chosen world we live. There is truth and meaning in all the words you will hear us say.

I gnorance is the part of us we accept that others cannot; stupidity is what we strive with all we are to overcome, between these two there is a great difference we know. Hear me now! When I say, "Ignorance is the lack of knowledge in truth of a matter. Stupidity is to have attained that knowledge and not put it where it should go!"

A ncestral disciplines when learned and practiced by a people of any nation in this universe we live within, when based upon a truth that hath no lie, "A Same Spirit, " leads to the return of truth to all nations in the infinite realm of all that is, was, and ever shall be; this is the truth of all truths, if you listen you will hear it.

N ation of the Nations "IkcheWashashi," the true hope of all Peoples, brought us... whom have learned to accept: we have all had 'Different Lives' many times been here before. So we must quest for a vision of who we are; by whom we were, in the Old Ancestral Way, as we know is true. In the silent darkness alone for each, it is made clear.

"OYATE NINKTE WACIN YELO"   HO!   ~HOKA WANAGI~

Used with permission by Jeremiah Ja'n Selogy

A Message from the Wintu Tribe

Condensed for full description please visit their website
www.winnememwintu.us/

"We come from Mount Shasta, and our sacred spring that
runnels through Panther Meadows is our genesis place. It is
truly a sacred place, and unfortunately many outsiders, who
don't understand how to behave there, are drawn to it.

The spring in Mt. Shasta's Panther Meadows is where we
first bubbled into the world at the time of creation.

☐ Do not deposit anything in the spring whether it be
crystals, ashes or anything else. We cannot heal sacred
lands; sacred lands heal us.

☐ Do not built anything in the meadows or leave anything
behind. It's perfect as the Creator made it. You can't
improve it.

☐ Do not visit the meadows in large groups

☐ Do not bring other indigenous-inspired religious Items on Mt. Shasta.

☐ If visiting the meadow, be sure to stay on the stepping stones. The trampling of the grass can damage the small tunnels dug by creatures that allows the spring to bubble throughout the meadow.

☐ If the meadow is sacred to you, do not hesitate to pass along these instructions to others

☐ Mt. Shasta is effectively our church. We would not go into a stranger's cathedral, light the sacred fire and start a ceremony. We ask that you provide us the same respect."

There are also many other faiths.

Buddhist Shasta Abbey 3724 Summit Drive, Est 1971

Mt Shasta, CA 96067

A Catholic presence was established when the Italian settlers arrived in the early 1900s to work in the mills.

St Anthony 507 Pine Street Mt. Shasta,

Mt Shasta hosts those of many differing faiths and has many churches of Christian, Native American, as well as those of New Age beliefs throughout the City.

Chapter 3

THE LEMURIANS?   BIGFOOT?   FOLKLORE?

In order to understand the legend of the Lemurians it is important to follow the trail back to the legends' true origins. This may surprise you!

In the 1880s a Siskiyou County, California, resident named Frederick Spencer Oliver wrote *A Dweller on Two Planets, or, the Dividing of the Way,* which described a secret city inside of Mount Shasta, and he mentioned 'Lemuria'.

The book claimed that there were survivors from a sunken continent called Lemuria that were living in or on Mount Shasta.

Oliver claimed the Lemurians lived in a complex of tunnels beneath the mountain. He also claimed that they were seen walking the surface dressed in white robes. Later writings of Guy Ballard and the Great White Brotherhood,

Summit Lighthouse, and others strengthened the belief in Lemuria at Mt Shasta.

Edgar Lucian Larkin, a writer and astronomer, wrote in 1913 an article in which he reviewed the Oliver book. The Lemuria-Mount Shasta legend has developed into one of Mount Shasta's most prominent legends

Accordingly, Frederick Spencer Oliver was a Yrekan teen who claimed that his hand began to uncontrollably write a manuscript dictated to him by Phylos, a Lemurian spirit.

The author claims to have written most of the novel within sight of Mount Shasta, and autobiographical telling of the story from Phylos the Thibetan's point of view is an interesting twist.

I quote from the book,

> "See, as I saw, not with the vision of flesh, the walls, polished as by jewelers, though excavated as by giants; floors carpeted with long, fleecy gray fabric that looked like fur, but was a mineral product; ledges intersected by the builders, and in their wonderful polish exhibiting veining of gold, or silver, or green copper ores, and maculations of precious stones.
>
> Verily, a mystic temple, made a far from the adding crowd, a refuge whereof those who,
>
> "Seeing, see not," can truly say: "And no man knows***
> "And no man saw it e'er."
>
> Once I was there, friend, casting pebbles in the stream's deep pools; yet it was then hid, for only a few are privileged.
>
> And departing, the spot was forgotten, and today, unable as any one who reads this, I cannot tell its place.

Curiosity will never unlock that secret. Does it truly exist?

Seek and ye shall find; knock and it shall be opened unto you. Shasta is a true guardian and silently towers, giving no sign of that within his breast.

But there is a key.

The one who first conquers self, Shasta will not deny.

This is the last scene. You have viewed the proud peak both near and far; by day, by night; in the smoke, and in the clear mountain air; seen its interior, and from its apex gazed upon it and the globe stretched away 'neath your feet.

'Tis a sight of God's handiwork, sublime, awful, never-to-be-forgotten; and as thy soul hath sated itself with admiration thereof,
in that measure be now filled with His Peace."

I especially like the quote about the key. That is the KEY to finding all the mystery of Shasta! One must conquer self!

In 1925 a writer by the name of Selvius wrote "Descendants of Lemuria: A Description of an Ancient Cult in America" which was published in the *Mystic Triangle*, Aug., 1925 and which was entirely about the mystic Lemurian village at Mount Shasta.

Selvius claims that Professor Edgar Lucian Larkin viewed the Lemurian site on Mount Shasta using his telescope: quoted,

"Even no less a careful investigator and scientist than Prof. Edgar Lucin Larkin, for many years director of Mount Lowe Observatory, said in newspaper and magazine articles that he had seen, on many occasions, the great temple of this mystic village, while gazing through a long-distance telescope."

In 1931, Wisar Spenle Cerve wrote *Lemuria: the lost continent of the Pacific*

Cerve's book, published by the Ancient Mystical Order Rosae Crucis, has provided the popular description of the Lemurians as "tall, graceful, and agile," and as visitors that "would come to one of the smaller towns and trade nuggets and gold dust for some modern commodities"

James Bramwell also described Lemuria in his book, *Lost Atlantis*, as "a continent that occupied a large part of what is now the South Pacific Ocean."

He described the people of Lemuria in detail and attributed them with being one of the "root-races of humanity." He claims Lemurians are the ancestors of the Atlanteans, who survived the period "of the general racial decadence which affected the Lemurians in the last stages of their evolution."

Above quoted in part from Lemurian Folklore; Wikipedia Section

And thus began the Legends and Lore of the Lemurians of Mt Shasta!

One might say that the information is based upon channeled information and lore, but thousands of people come here every year to connect with Lemurians and the ancient culture of Lemuria

As for myself, I can say this;

"I had no knowledge of Lemuria or Lemurians, when I first came to Mt Shasta in November of 1999. I had never even heard of Lemurians! Yet, I met 'Adam'namos', High Priest of the Lemurians here at Mt Shasta. It changed my life."

I have written four books about that encounter with the Lemurians starting with my first book, *"On Assignment With Adama."* I have been in contact for the last *fifteen years.* The information has always been accurate and precise. I used to get latitude and longitude coordinates with a command, "Go here!" That has happened 36 times! My 'assignments' were completed.

When I went home to NH to my Elders in 1999, I was told of the legend of the White Mountains of NH where the White Spirit Beings would one day arise to save the earth from destruction; hence the 'White Mountains.' They were waiting too.

I found the Lemurian site in New Hampshire when I returned, just where Adama told me it would be. Lemurians? They are *REAL!* What are they? I believe they are Spirit, The Ancient Ones, seeking to help humanity.   *Susan Isabelle*

**An Ancient Maya Head Sculpture? At Mount Shasta?
I wonder what that's doing here? Maybe it has to do
with the Maya 13th Crystal Skull living here?
About 30 feet high, it faces the mountain!**

So, I will Tell You My Favorite Lemurian Tale

I was in the area known on Mount Shasta as 'Sand Flats' in 2006, camping. It was late afternoon and I was out by the ledges. I was far away from any other campsites or people.

Having come to seek a vision on the mountain in the solitude, I wanted to relax. I took out my paints, easel and I set up a canvas. I sat down and was just about to place the brush of paint onto the canvas. Then, I heard a woman singing nearby.

It startled me and I shouted out, "Who's there?" All was silent. I looked around the campsite and there was not a sound or being anywhere. I sat down again and started to smear the paint onto the canvas once again. The singing began again! This time, I held very, very still, my hand still holding the brush to the canvas. I held my breath!

The sound was coming from just in front of me, between two trees, but there was no one there! The song was beautiful, soft and repetitive, singing, *"Oh Sau an ney   a sau ....who na nee".*   It was in an a woman's voice in a Native tongue, but I did not recognize the song at all.

Relaxing in the beauty of the song, I asked gently not with words but with my mind only, "Who are you?"

"I am the Woman of the Mountain." She replied. " I would like you to paint my portrait."

Her words came to my mind as clear spoken words. I was shocked! Inwardly I gasped, but I remained absolutely still. I tried to think quickly. I replied.

"My Lady, I would love to do that for you, but I cannot see you."

"That is alright, may I take your hand?" She asked.

"Yes!" With that my hand was covered in a soft glow, warm and gentle. It was so loving that I had no fear at all!

My brush began to move of its own. The paints spread easily over the canvas and the form of a woman between two trees appeared. I watched my hand paint. I was fascinated as I watched her form appear. The older, Lady was gently , prayerfully, holding the earth. The entire time The Lady of the Mountain sang her song,

"Oh Sau an ney   a sau ....who na nee."

Soon the painting was completed. The song faded away along with the glowing form over my hand. The sun was setting as I stood and walked over to the edge of the cliff. The song began once again.   But this time as the sun set The Lady and I sang the song together…

A Lemurian Song;

"Oh Sau an ney a sau ..who na knee... a na.... sauuu ...ah na

sau...   A way.... away ... a... way,......

ha.. na ...h a na ....a ...way,   ma... naa......ma.. na...ha...naaa

Interpreted "o'sau-means, " In the Future",

Na nee means, "One who is graced with God's favor".

Ha na- means "Happiness" a-way, means "coming/going"
ma naaa means   "The Guiding Light- Nourishment"

So you could interpret the song to mean,

"In the future, one who is graced with God's favor, is
happy at the coming and receives The Guiding Light
(food for the soul)"

You may hear me sing it on youtube- Susan Isabelle Sings

Susan Isabelle 2004 when she first arrived at Mount Shasta commissioned the painting of Adama

I have written several books regarding that encounter with the Lemurian High Priest and now write to you so you too may have your own experiences.

May you find enlightenment.

Now, I Will Share A Big Foot Tale

I met a Native gentleman that had lived at the mountain for over thirty five years. He prefers that I not use his name, so let it suffice to know that he has a great deal of knowledge. I asked him if I might accompany him deep into the forest to the vision quest ledges at some future time.

That is the place where the Native peoples went to seek their vision and purpose in life. He'd already had someone that he was taking within the week, so I was invited to go along also.

This is in a very secret location, a holy place on the mountain. No one just enters this area, it is a very great gift to do so and physically, ten years later, I am now unable to make the trip anymore. Here one may see the past carved into stone. Evidence of structures and an ancient way of life may also be seen. Shapes of creatures gaze out from stones as you pass by. Lemuria!

Please, if you ever encounter any of these stone sculptures, they are not there for you to take. Leave everything as you see it. There are consequences if you disturb them.

Squaw Meadow is such an example of this; look- do not disturb! Go with this thought and the mountain will show you her secret wonders! Remember, you must overcome yourself! Others are blinded.

As we walked along, he pointed out the tracks of large footprints. We spoke about Bigfoot and he told me stories of the families they have, of children and their peaceful way of life. It is such a shame that all humanity can think about is getting one for a trophy and proof of their existence.

He told me they will only show themselves to those that are of pure intention and peace. Apparently, once an official person had entered this area and was literally run off the mountain. He never wanted to return! Normally, they hide from us but they will defend their families if they perceive a threat.

That night as we sat around the campfire we could see the pathway leading down to the ledges in firelight. Suddenly, it seemed as if the tress were glowing. "Look!" he whispered," The Bigfoot, they are here!"

I could make out tall figures that were glowing white, standing behind the trees. They were peering out from behind the trees at us! I want everyone to know that I do not use altering drugs or herbs in any form. They were standing behind the trees! I saw them! But, you say, aren't Bigfoot big hairy creatures? When they want to frighten you off they are, but in their true form, they glow as the sun!

"Be still!" He commanded us. The three of us sat motionless until the glowing beings left us. "That was unusual." He stated. "They don't usually show themselves to people." He looked more closely at us.

"They are the *Sacred Whites, the Guardians of Shasta.* They know me because I have lived with them on this mountain; once they came into my camp. There was a whole family of them and they wanted me to go with them, but I was not ready."

When we bedded down for the night I could hear them walking around the campsite. We were definitely being checked out!

The next day he asked me to accompany him on a walk in the forest. We covered a lot of ground at a fast pace that day before he finally began to slow down.

"Susan, just look to your right; don't say anything." He commanded me. I glanced to my right side and about twenty feet away there was a Bigfoot mother with her child! They were walking with us!

29

I instantly felt a connection to them in my heart. The feeling was almost overwhelming as I was filled with love!

"Oh," I whispered, "I just want to tell them that I love them! I wish I could hug her!"

"Susan, don't do that!" He said quickly to me. " Keep walking, they already know that or they wouldn't be here with us! They just want *you* to know."

The two bigfoot continued with us for quite some time. I sent loving thoughts to the two of them as I walked until finally, they disappeared into the forest!

I so wish people would stop trying to prove everything and simply be and love. Then the doors of Spirit will open to humanity. Isn't it a shame that other beings have to hide from us?

Just a quick note to you about consequences;

One of my students that knew better, went up on the mountain into one of the sacred areas. She saw two huge pine cones. She wanted them. She picked them up and put them into the trunk of her car. She " felt guilty about doing it" she later told me, "but I wanted them."

She and her husband then drove up to the upper parking lot on Shasta. Under a clear blue sky, hail began pelting her-not her husband or anyone else- but just her!

"I know! I know!" She shouted to the sky. "Hurry John, I have to put them back!"

They drove back down the mountain and replaced the fairy's pine cones exactly where they had been taken. Remember; Do not take what is not yours. If something is given to you, honor the source and give thanks.

CHAPTER 4
YES,THIS IS SACRED LAND

Middle Falls, McCloud. Yes, Mount Shasta is very sacred. It is one of the most sacred places on the Earth.

Many pilgrims seeking enlightenment come to Shasta as a part of their global pilgrimage to the other sacred mountains of the Earth. She stands in sacredness as her sisters across the Earth. Let's take a look at where other people travel to find their enlightenment. Sooner or later they will arrive at Mount Shasta as she does call them and you, here. You may find yourself being called to one of these too after your time at Shasta. Many do.

Mount Kailash, China/Tibet

Thousands of Buddhist, Hindu, Jain and Bonpo pilgrims journey to the remote Himalayan town of Darchen each year to make koras, ritual circuits, around the base of Mount Kailash. Setting foot on the mountain is considered to be a sacrilege, but to near the base is believed to erase a lifetime of sins

31

Or Mount Hebron in Israel; **Mount Sinai** "Moses' Mountain" or "Mount Moses"; הר סיני also known as **Mount Horeb**, is a mountain in the Sinai of Egypt, the biblical place where Moses received the Ten Commandments.

Mount Fuji, Japan

This snowcapped mountain west of Tokyo is sacred in both Buddhism and Shintoism. During the July and August climbing season more than 200,000 people hike to the top of this 12,388 ft. peak. Mount Fuji has been venerated as the home of a fire god, a Shinto goddess and Dainichi Nyorai, the Great Sun Buddha

Mount Agung, Bali

The Balinese consider the volcanic Mount Agung to be the center of the universe. It rises 10,308 feet high in eastern Bali. The Mother Temple of Besakih, the largest and holiest temple in Bali, sits roughly 3,000 feet up its slopes

Mount Everest, Nepal/China border

Tibetans call Mount Everest the Goddess Mother of the Universe, the Nepalese call it Goddess of the Sky. At 29,029 feet, it is the highest mountain on the planet.

Mount Nebo, Jordan

According to the final chapter of Deuteronomy, Mount Nebo is where the Hebrew prophet Moses beheld the Promised Land. On a clear day you can see the Dead Sea, Bethlehem, Jerusalem, the River Jordan, Jericho and the Mount of Olives.

Mount Croagh Patrick, Ireland

As many as one million pilgrims trek this peak annually to pray at the Stations of the Cross, participate in Mass, or just enjoy the spectacular view over Ireland's western coast. Pre-Christian Celts believed the deity Crom Dubh lived on the mountain and later St. Patrick who introduced Christianity to Ireland is believed to have spent 40 days and nights fasting and praying atop the mountain

The San Francisco Peaks, Arizona

More than a dozen Native American tribes consider this volcanic chain in the Coconino National Forest to be sacred, including the Hopi, who believe the peaks are the mythological home of the Kachina People. The highest point in Arizona; 12,633 feet.

Popocatepel, Southeast of Mexico City In both Aztec and Nahua legends. Called El Popoâ ,• for short, is a living, breathing entity.14 Spanish monasteries on El Popoâ slopes were built in 16th century, it is a UNESCO World Heritage Site.

<u>Hawaii</u> The volcanoes of Mauna Kea on the island of *Hawaii* and Haleakala on Maui were sacred mountains to the Polynesians and pilgrims still climb them today.

Other locations;
<u>Ayers Rock</u> is also known by its Aboriginal name 'Uluru'. It is a sacred part of Aboriginal creation mythology, or dreamtime. - Reality being a dream. Uluru is a large magnetic mound not unlike **Silbury Hill** in England, and it is also located on a major planetary gridline.

Machu Picchu of Peru, the Pyramids of Egypt,

The Pyramids of Tikal and in Belize, the home of the Crystal Skulls.

SO, WHY IS IT *SACRED* MOUNT SHASTA?

The Shadow Of An Angel In The Snow On Shasta- Sky Walker Photo

What Makes Mount Shasta so Sacred? What is different about her in comparison to the other sacred mountains of the Earth?

Mount Shasta has been identified in some writings as the " root chakra of the earth," but I have come to respect the energy of the mountain and see her more as a "heart center" for the earth. I have some personal thoughts about this that I'd like to share.

The heart center, or thymus chakra, is the place where we bring down from the higher realms Creator's Energy and secure it to ourselves; that secured Light produces our creative voice, that of higher thought and of our God Consciousness. That's what happens at Shasta for many people.

Beneath the thymus chakra we have the 'will center', or stomach chakra. There we suffer sometimes the stomach ailments and consequences of stressful decisions; decisions that tear us in two; that of higher decisions and that of earth bound obligations..

That is the dividing point in the human body of higher light decisions and that of survival choices and earth energies. Strength of will abides here.

Beneath that we have the navel, power center, soul connection and experience the creative powers that connect us to the 'root chakra-earth connection.'

I believe Mount Shasta is really the HEART CHAKRA.

In the Native American beliefs, it is the 'Genesis', where human creation occurred. It is where heaven came to earth to begin. The love of the Creator of All touched the earth to bring forth mankind, made in His / Her image. That is Love! Thought and Love come together here.

It is always a joy to meet people that will show me the little heart shaped stones that they find up on the mountain. It is as if the mountain produces these stones for her pilgrims!

We even have two heart-shaped lakes at the mountain! People

open their hearts at this mountain and seek a blessing from the Creator of All. Those that seek here will find that blessing.

There are many reasons for my personal belief about this, but perhaps the most obvious is the fact that Mount Shasta is actually Mt Shasta and Shastina, two major peaks; both male and female energies are present and combined in a sacred joining.

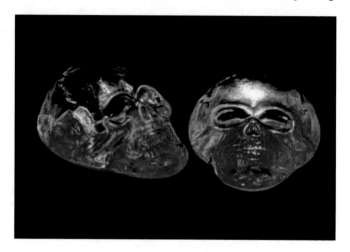

It is also the home of the 13th Crystal Skull, a male and a female, that come together to form a Sacred Heart

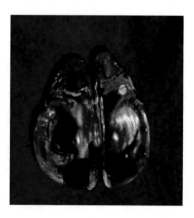

Two That Become One Heart

Chapter 5   Secure in the Heart

Even the motto of Mt Shasta City is "Heaven on Earth!"

It is a place where The Light of Heaven comes to Earth! It is male and female. It is as if a great 14,173 foot twin flame crystal rises up against the deep blue sky. That is bound to open one's heart! Open up and let the Light of Heaven enter!

Seeing her for the first time takes one breath away. It is magnificent, splendid in its might and power; but more so is its affect upon the soul of mankind.

Something very special happens here at Mt Shasta for some people, for others, well, not so much-and that is what this book is all about.

If you desire to find the spiritual side of Mt Shasta while you are here, there are some things you need to know. Many come and run about quickly; seeking for something they do not understand. Are you one of those?

Some want to experience the Lemurians, some want to see the UFO's that are here, others want to teach everyone else and cannot hear anything. Are you one of these?

Whatever, the mountain has its own rules. Some receive and others do not because they do not understand this mountain. The mountain will not receive them. You don't want to be one of those.

When I first arrived in Mt Shasta to live nearly ten years ago, I was puzzled by all the locals that would see me every few months. They would always ask me, somewhat startled, "Oh, you're still here?"

They seem to be surprised to see that I was still in the area. I can say that it came close a few times as the challenges to heart, mind and soul were part of a mountain purification process that I had not anticipated.

There were a few times I was ready to pack up a head back to the city. I laugh now but it wasn't funny when I discovered one February that I had rented a condo at the annual mating ground of the Lake Shastina skunks!

Twelve skunks were removed from beneath my condo on the waterfront and more were coming when I'd had enough! I bought a motorhome, packed up and I left the place back to nature's rule. Shasta had won that round!

Humanity must learn that it cannot take what is not theirs to take. Those mating grounds were there long before that condo was built! It *belonged* to the skunks. I had to learn a lesson.

I later came to understand that very few people seem to be able to actually live in the Mt Shasta area for one reason or another. Even those that come with means and money leave after a short time. It is also strange that our population here doesn't seem to rise above 4,000 people! It appears to be the same for each of the surrounding towns.

There are reasons for this. I once asked the Native American Elder, Charlie Thom, when he was still alive, a question;

"Charlie, why don't you live on the mountain?"

"Oh, no!" He exclaimed.

"Why not?" I pressed.

"That would be like living on the battery terminals!" His eyes grew big and astonished!

I laughed, but by then, I understood. Let me explain.

Painting of Charlie Red Hawk Thom, our friend and Elder, by unknown artist. It captures his fire spirit. It was given to us at his request, by his family at his passing.

Were it not for Charlie Red Hawk Thom, much of what you enjoy here Mount Shasta would not even exist. He worked tirelessly to ensure the forests were preserved, the rivers ran free and the Salmon were restored. We thank you Charlie!

With his establishing the first Earth Circle World Gathering at Panther Meadows in 1993, the Federal Government gave him the land for the ceremony. Effectively, after a 3 day sweat lodge purification ceremony on Mount Shasta, the Ghost Dance Proclamation of the 1800's forbidding this type of ceremony was made null and void within the halls of Congress and the US Government by this action.

To explain; Sacred mountains and vortex areas have an energy that serves the purpose of purifying humanity to allow the reconnection to their Creator, to reach higher consciousness. Mount Shasta has many such vortex locations. That is what a heart chakra does too. Fasting and prayer on the mountain? Oh, yes!

They serve to bring us to higher and higher levels of spiritual growth. The very elevation makes your head swim; not always for lack of oxygen, but because of unseen spiritual forces that watch.

To attain spiritual growth during one's lifetime, one must be ready to face all aspects of oneself.

That means that you will be required to see both your 'good qualities' and overcome your 'limitations.'

Then, your heart is opened and then, you must make a decision.

That means all of your secrets are laid bare to be self -examined in truth, plus the process of learning how to bring the Light of Healing to your soul. This is what Charlie was talking about when he said humanity must first be healed before right decisions can be processed and implemented.

I will share a story with you.

Mt Shasta BLVD and 101 West Lake St at the Shambhala Center

When I first arrived in Mount Shasta, I went to see Louise Jones, the author of the Telos book series. She and I spoke extensively of our encounters with Adama of the Lemurians. As she was a 'speaker' for Adama's message to humanity, I was 'on assignment' with him to assist humanity.

To come into her area and to be at peace, it was important that I speak to her. By honoring her in this way, the most unexpected thing happened for me.

After we spoke and bonded, she was a wonderful person, she asked me to watch her out door book table while she spoke at the College of the Siskiyous in Weed the following week. I agreed to help her set up.

On that beautiful sunny day while she was inside speaking, I watched a tall, handsome man stride across the green lawn.

As he drew near a strong gust of wind lifted all of Aurelas' hundreds of papers and brochures, blowing them over the railing and depositing them directly at his feet.

We both ran about picking up the papers and placed them back on her table. Afterwards, he asked me where I had come from, I told him I had just arrived from the northeast to live in Shasta.

As he was picking up a few papers from under and around the table, I asked him why he had come; he looked up at me and answered, "I've come here for you." He meant it. We are still together, now ten years later.

Remember that one act of kindness may have untold benefits. But the story goes on from here.

I asked him that day if he knew where I could find the Native American Elder for the area, Charlie Thom. I would need to see him next. He knew exactly where Charlie was; they were friends.

Even as the Wintu state in their list, you don't go into someone else's church and do ceremony. I had come to do ceremony with the Crystal Skull in his backyard and I needed to speak to him, just as I had Louise. I needed to ask permission to do "medicine."

There are rules for human conduct. There are rules of respect. Humanity as a whole has stepped out on respect. No one understands this it seems. It causes a lot of problems for humanity. Charlie was a true Master, respect of souls was a key.

Souls interact (speak to one another) on the highest levels, whether or not we understand that. I am not speaking of the 'higher self teaching' or that of something 'outside of us', but our soul; of being an 'aware-soul.' There are consequences or benefits, to our own souls that are a result of that interaction and our own subsequent decisions we make in the physical.

Spoken or unspoken, the soul knows. When you close your eyes tonight you will enter the realm of spirit consciousness, your soul. There you may meet a fellow human spirit and discuss a path you each need to follow to attain a higher level of physical reality. You agree in that realm to assist one another in some way on a path to understanding of self. We help each other.

The next morning you arise and go out to shop for the day. You bump into the night-spirit-person in the physical and cause him to drop his groceries all over the floor!

Remember; during the night you had set the scenario; this accident was designed for you to meet, you were to pick up the cans together-BUT, a *decision* is made by you and you shout, "Why don't you watch where you're going!" You stomp out and loose the opportunity.

We do this all the time! We are not aware of our soul agreements and our limitations sometimes overrule the agreements. I encourage the Traveler to move slowly through life, to examine every moment, every dream, for the connective thread. It's there for us to discover. Learn respect for you may even be speaking to an angel that has come to assist you. Jesus said it best, "The spirit is willing but the flesh is weak."

At Mount Shasta, everything is magnified with the energy a thousand times over. Things happen very quickly here, so quickly that every moment can change and bring an opportunity to grow-if you are aware- if you are following Spirit!

This Cherokee prayer is recommended;
"Oh Great Spirit, help me always to speak the truth quietly,
to listen with an open mind when others speak,
and to remember the peace that may be found in silence."

43

Sometime later, we made the trip out to find Charlie. On that day, we made the drive to Quartz Valley near Fort Jones. We first stopped in a quarry area to sing Native American songs. We were drumming and singing *Bear Spirit* when a rickety truck drove up and a little man hopped out.

He came running up to us. "Well, I haven't worn this necklace in a long time!" He stated smiling broadly while showing us his big bear claw necklace. "I got I had to wear it today! Just who are you anyway?" He laughed hysterically, gleefully.

A spiritually evolved person, he knew we were coming. His soul told him. He even dressed for the occasion to match our song! How's that for soul-talk! Oh, to be that spiritually awake all the time like Charlie was in the physical and is now in the spirit!

He and Jeremiah were great friends and had been for a long time. We followed him back to his house where we spent the afternoon talking.

I told him the about The Maya 13ᵗʰ Skull, the Sacred Heart, and that I needed to secure the ascension energies in 2012 to fulfill prophecy, and some of what I would need to do while I was in Mt Shasta. Humanity's welfare was a stake. But, I needed his blessing. The flow of energy must be without any strife.

This is an important piece to know; whenever you are about to do something, you need to be able to prepare the flow of good energy in as much peacefulness as possible. Your heart needs to be open and free to accept the flow from the Creator. Respect is a part of this; respect of people, places, and things.

Otherwise, all is based on not-right thinking. We become influenced by the lower aspects of self and as mentioned before, 'become incapable of making good decisions.' People wonder why nothing works out for them?

Then, the bargain was struck; one does not enter here without a payment. I was about to do big medicine, there was to be an equal exchange. An *equal exchange*, I said. The balance must be kept.

That is also a Universal Law and Truth the Traveler must know and acknowledge. Do you go into an area expecting to take from it or go into an area and try to give to it? Are you supposed to? Do you even give it thought?

Remember what the Wintu said? They reminded us that the mountain is perfect just the way Creator made it, just the way it is. We can't do anything to it or heal it.

So why do you come? Come here to worship, honor the Creator, Mother Earth, seek a vision, or a mission vision.

Anything else must be thought out in great detail and only with Great Spirit's guidance in service to humanity. It must all be kept in balance. That's what I was doing at this moment with the Karuk Elder Charlie Red Hawk Thom.

But, what? What could I give in return?

"Charlie," Jeremiah spoke, "is there was something you would want to do but cannot do right now? Somewhere you'd want to go? Something that you think we could do for you- what would that be?"

"Yes, yes, there is something that needs to be done. Will you do it for me?" He anxiously asked us looking back and forth at each of us.

"Yes," we both answered.

"I need you to go to Arizona and clean up a big mess for me." Charlie spoke softly with great sadness. "A big mess! Evil has come there. It can't come any further west."

He was pleading to us to go from his soul. Obviously, we'd discussed this in dream soul time. He knew, but I didn't remember all the details. Charlie was a true Master of Soul-Talk.

He looked up at us, hopefully. "You'll know when you get there. You'll be guided." He promised, he reminded me.

He could read our minds and he knew what he was asking us to do just like he knew we were coming. 'Soul-talk!'

"Arizona?" I thought to myself. "Why, I hardly know this man, and who is this Jeremiah?" We looked at each other. He was thinking the same thing about me.

"Yes, Charlie, I'll go!" Jeremiah and I said it at the same time. The 'decision' choice, was confirmed. The need for humanity was greater than our personal limitations; we had both decided to take up the challenge.

To trust in God for direction, for guidance and for the good of humanity is our soul's greatest school of earth- learning.

"Good! Then you must leave right NOW!" Charlie jumped straight up into the air, spun, screamed something and hit us both with lightning bolts. "**Go Now!**"

We nearly ran out of the house to be on our way. At the end of the road leading out from his house it began to hail. We looked at one another, "We're going to have our hands full." Jeremiah said.

Also, Misun Jeremiah's dog in the back seat, had found a skunk to play with. As soon as possible, we'd need to wash the dog!

Talk about a challenge, an eight hundred mile journey with a skunky dog!

Yes, there was going to be a lot of oppositional energy on this trip. We were on a sacred mission to stop something that was evil and the Karuk Elder of Mt Shasta expected us to be able to handle this. Susan, Jeremiah and Charlie had all agreed-somewhere in time. My head was spinning. That's how Mount Shasta is-always.

He had made it clear that this evil may come to Shasta and all the way to the coast if not stopped. My ability to work with the skulls at Mt Shasta also depended upon a good relationship with the powers of the area, and they had to be clear and pure.

Now, we were on our way! Before we knew it we were driving deep into the desert of Arizona. The expanse of road in a certain area began to swim before my eyes. I could sense the Ancient Ones calling to me, pulling on my spirit.

"There is great power here, I feel it. Someone wishes to speak." I told Jeremiah.

He'd never seen me go into trance like this before. He hardly even knew me. I resisted as long as I could but the voice was powerful.

"There is an Ancient One here, Jeremiah." I spoke. "He is telling me we must not go into to sleep in Sedona; to go south, we will be too vulnerable."

I paused and looked over at Jeremiah. He was listening. I continued.

"He says, "the power is too great; we must watch for the sign." Then, I could feel he was pulling his spirit back from me and then, the message I had heard, was over. There would be no more.

"What sign?" Jeremiah asked me curiously; unsure about this woman he was with- possibly another soul-talker?

"I don't know, but there will be a sign and we must follow it." I said firmly. "And we are not to sleep in Sedona."

As we drew nearer to our destination, we stopped for gas at a station. I sat in the car while Jeremiah went inside to get supplies. After a few minutes I got out of the car just to stretch my legs.

Then I noticed something really, really strange.

At the next pump over there was an average looking man. He had taken the gas hose from off the side of the pump. He started the gas running, but was not putting it into the car. He was leaning over with the flowing gas hose down toward the ground.

I looked closer around the pump, just to see this more clearly.

The gas was running, flowing out of the hose. It was as if he had a gas can beneath, but *there was no gas can*! The gas simply disappeared into air!

I looked up and saw Jeremiah in the store. I ran in to get him. "Jeremiah! Jeremiah! The sign! It's here! You have to speak to that man- over there!"

I pointed and Jeremiah, seeing the spectacle at the gas pump, quickly went over to speak to the man. I stood back as they spoke. The man hung up his gas hose. The two men parted.

"Get in!" he commanded me a few moments later as he jumped into the car. "We're going to follow him!"

Both cars sped off in a new direction, down a dirt path and across a desert field. I hung the Crystal Skull around my neck. It has proven to be very protective before. I felt I was going to really need it now.

We arrived. Somewhere in the desert we had stopped. There was nothing around for miles and all I could see was the horizon. Getting out of the cars we stood facing one another. The man spoke first

"This place, it is my land." He said it almost in an apologizing way. "This is my son," he said nodding toward a teenage boy standing beside him. "The creek that runs down by here".....he hesitated... "washed away about three feet of soil from the creek walls. It's at a depth that I've never seen before in all my life."

He paused and I could see fear in him. "There are some ancient petroglyphs, native symbols all down there, that are now exposed. I'll show them to you."

I took out my walking staff from out of the back of the car. The man looked at it curiously but said nothing. Jeremiah took out his drum and the dog, Misun.

We silently walked down a path toward a creek. The air became dense and even the dog hung back as we neared the water.

My hair began to stand on end and it was cold, very cold in this place where it must have been 90 degrees under the sun.

Across the water on the other side of the creek, the creek wall was holding back something, something very sinister and dark. I felt my chest tighten. I would go no further.

"Come, Misun", Jeremiah called. The nervous, panting dog dropped to the ground. He wasn't going over there either. "OK then, I'll go alone."

I watched Jeremiah jump the rocks to the other side. He dropped to his knees and began to drum and sing powerful, ancient songs. They were songs I'd never heard before.

There was movement in the air; it was a little easier to breathe. The man spoke to me with hesitation, "I saw symbols-symbols just like those on your staff over there." He seemed to be afraid of my staff.

I looked down at my staff. "Oh! Yes, these are *protection symbols*. They are on my staff to help me in these- these- situations." I pointed to the creek wall. "Likely they were placed on the wall of the creek to keep back the forces there, to keep them contained."

"Can we have them?" the man asked me while nodding at his son. His son nodded back at his father, then at me. They were both scared nearly half to death of this place.

"Yes, come over here." I placed the staff with the symbols over them and chanted the ancient names and prayers of protection. Soon their bodies relaxed and they both sighed in relief. Their bodies too had been cleared of this evil presence. Something had happened here to these men.

Standing now we could literally feel that the work Jeremiah had done. With his songs and prayers he had cleared the entire place! The dog was up and dancing in the water joyfully when Jeremiah hopped back over the creek bed toward us.

"There! That should do it!" He was very happy. We were too. The man and his son were now smiling.

"Whatever had been released with the water washing away the protective field is now contained back in its place." He said as we got back in the car.

"Maybe that's what Charlie was talking about?" I asked, but already knew the answer; we still had to go south of Sedona and we were expected to stay there.

"I don't think so," he replied as we got back on the highway.

I didn't either, but whatever the containment of that force we'd just experienced had something to do with our trip.

I'm going to interrupt this story for a moment. How much do you really want to be 'spiritual'? How brave are you? Are you willing to face the fact that we are not all one? That there is really evil-that which hates the Light and all goodness? Have you examined what you've been taught?

This book is for the spiritual traveler, the one that is on a path to enlightenment. You absolutely cannot be 'spiritual' until you do understand this. Why do you think Archangel Michael has a sword? WHY WOULD HE HAVE A SWORD? Yes, the Light is all forgiving, but some-they don't want it.

God does not force anyone, but I can tell you that time is coming to an end. Light will be Light and darkness will remain dark-forever separated by IT'S OWN WILL and desire to be so.

Until then, it is our responsibility to forward the Light of Love and forgiveness so all may enter the Kingdom of Light that so desire it. Many are held captive by the delusions of this world and those that seek control of our every thought.

As you can see in this story, to be aware of the soul-talk agreements allowed for everything to flow as it was supposed to. Meeting Jeremiah, Charlie, The Bear necklace, Jeremiah listening to my message, the man at the pump, all had to be in perfect flow.

Note; People always want miracles, but are stopped mid-way by their own preconceptions or trying to control everything. Spiritual Traveler, get out of your own way!

We were both exhausted. We found a secluded place, slept in the car to regain our strength, then were guided to the town of (to protect the people there I will not name it. They have suffered enough.)

As Jeremiah and I walked the little town, we stood close by one another. Quickly, we got back into the car. People approached the car, tapping on the windows. This was scary. These were zombies.

"Keep the window rolled up, Susan!" Jeremiah commanded.

Looking into the coal black eyes of the people we could see that their souls had been bound. Like walking zombies they went about their day to day activities, but there was a coldness, deep and forbidding that kept us far from them, and them from the ability to connect with us, in order to free them.

"What are we going to do, Jeremiah? We can't leave them like this!" I was near tears. "How can anyone-anything, be so cruel to humanity?"

"This is the binding of souls-it is all about harvesting and binding of souls for POWER!" He angrily responded. "This is what Charlie was afraid would come to Shasta and to the West!"

"What can we do?" I asked again.

"Let's go just outside of town. We need to think, to seek

guidance."

We drove twenty or so miles away to a secluded area in the desert. No one was around. We pulled off the road at an opening with a steep bank below. We'd be safe here, we thought. We sat there for a while, praying.

Then, Jeremiah got out of the car and looked around. I joined him. We looked over the banking on the steeper side. We could see that there was a yellow tape extended across saying, "Do not enter this area." That was strange, as there appeared to be nothing around for miles.

Could it be that Spirit had led us directly to the place we needed to be? Apparently so, I watched as Jeremiah began to descend down the embankment. He knelt to pray and to drum his amazing Native dispelling the darkness, songs.

I stood guard with the dog while holding my staff and Crystal Skulls of the Maya.

After a few minutes a car gently drove in behind our car. A man timidly got out of his car. "We need your protection." He simply stated to me.

I nodded. He stood quietly and I placed my staff in his hands. I asked God's blessing and protection for him.

Then another car came with six people. I did the same for them, then another car full and another until the whole side of the road was filled with the town's people, men, women, and children. All were standing in a big semi-circle around me and Jeremiah who was still drumming below.

I continued to pass the staff and bless the people. We all prayed. They began to smile.

We all watched as a mist was lifting from the earth just beyond Jeremiah; souls of the dead now rose from their bondage. Bundled and placed here in the desert, the people were held captive. Even the dead.

Do such things really exist? Oh, yes, they do.

It is time you become aware!

Hiding your head will not make it go away

Thinking positively will not make it go away

After a few more minutes it appeared that the whole town had arrived, but there was one more car coming; crazily he flew into the area, jumped out and began running toward the crowd!

"You can do this! You can't do this!" He screamed!

The people interlocked their arms to form a barrier around us. The crazed man beat on them, screaming at us, but they stood strong! Someone with great authority said, "Leave!" the man slunk away. He had been defeated. This was over. Power had returned to the people!

As Jeremiah came up from the embankment, he was surprised to see all the joyful, smiling people that had gathered there. The little children ran up and hugged him and he swept them up into his arms. The people thanked us; they and their loved ones were now free. Slowly, they thanked us and got back into their cars.

Before they all left, a woman asked if she may take this picture for us. It is the only one I have of this day. I am grateful to God.

"Look there!" He pointed at something in the distance. He was pointing to a distant mesa. "The souls of the dead are being assembled-right there."

It looked like a cloud- like 'ship' was gathering the mist-like souls.

"They'll be taken home now, after some healing." He said softly.

I thanked God that we'd been shown how to help. He stood still for a moment; I could see that he was listening to Spirit. "We can go now, but first I need to go up there."

I watched him climb up over the other side of the road. As he came down he was holding something in his hand.

"Spirit told me that this is for you!" With a big smile, he held out a rock and I took it. As I turned it over, inside the rock was a big, beautiful blue, Arizona opal!

That was then I realized we would always be together. In front of me stood the one that had been promised. This was the 'Protector' Spirit had promised to send to protect me and help me when I left the Northeast. I was to do much work in the

West! I could already see that I needed his help. But more than all of this, I knew I was falling in love with this very unusual man. (Note; For those of you that have read my other books, Richard's true spirit left the body to care in 2004. Before he left he told me the protector was coming-remember, Cosmic Eve Book III)

We went south of Sedona as instructed for a good night's rest. The next morning, we made the drive into town. We wanted to have breakfast, but we could not find a parking place anywhere. Back and forth we drove up and down the main street. Nothing!

Suddenly two black ravens were flying beside our car, one on each side of the car. "Jeremiah! Those are my nature spirit guides! They are flying with us! Watch where they go!" I shouted.

Instantly the two ravens left the sides of our car and flew together in front of our windshield. Incredibly, we watched as the two turned into *three* ravens they veered to the left, up a hill.

"Follow them!" I was excited now. They were leading us.

He made the sharp left up the hill and we followed the ravens into a parking area. We stopped the car to see just where they had led us. And then, it began to hail!

It was hailing so hard that Jeremiah moved the car underneath a tree to protect us. "I think we're here, but we can't get out of the car." He said, frustrated.

"Wait, I can do something." I prayed and formed a small ball of light between my hands. Once formed, I blew it upward through the roof of the car.

Instantly the hail stopped and the sunshine returned. Jeremiah looked at me strangely. We were both learning a lot about one another.

We got out of the car to see exactly where we were. We were in a vortex area. My little light ball had dissipated the darkness. The hail was an attempt to prevent us from our work, but darkness still hung heavy in the air. Something definitely was not right here.

Looking around we could see that we were high on a plateau by some trees. He took out his drum and without a word began to head down toward the thicker growth of trees. Jeremiah was set to do something about this situation.

Once again, the dog and I decided to hang back; this was a man's job after all…

As he was drumming the dog began pacing, pacing, running back and forth, frantically. Soon he was foaming at the mouth and growling at things unseen to my eyes, but I sure felt it! This was horrible!! I prayed for Jeremiah to have strength, prayed and prayed!

Then I noticed something; cars were flying up a back road that was almost hidden from my view. Men and teenage boys were jumping out of the cars, gathering and shouting at one another! They were very, very mad. They formed a group, a mob of wild men!

Then, the mob began to move all together, heading up through the thick trees, coming up, all heading toward Jeremiah! They were making noises like growling, there was screaming and cursing!

He was oblivious to this as he was deep into his trance songs to dispel the wickedness here!

Misun, wildly barking and foaming charged down the hill toward the men!

I jumped in the car and crazily drove it into the woods crashing over brush. "Get in Jeremiah! Get in!" I screamed. "They're coming to get you!" I flung open the car's door.

He woke to his senses just as the men were closing in on us. "Misun! Get in!" He commanded as they jumped in the car together.

I sped furiously down the plateau as the angry mob cursed us as they ran after us from behind. They could do nothing now.

Once safe, "Did you get it?" I asked breathlessly.

"Yes, this is over." He said. "That's what it was back there-that was the place that they set this all up!" He stated, referring to the angry mob. I needed an explanation; my face spoke it to him.

"They were a part of a Lodge that went to the dark; I saw the sign. They've been binding the souls here, using the powers of darkness, but not anymore- *This House Is Clean*!!"

There is more to this story, but by now you can see that spiritual travelers are in a different world than the rest of the people.

A Spiritual Traveler is a Guardian for the people.

They go about doing good works- God's work!

Once back in Mount Shasta, we headed straight up the mountain. Together we began to sing and thank God for all that had happened. A great evil had been stopped!

As we drummed and prayed our thanks to the Creator, a huge, deep blue round vortex in the sky developed. It was surrounded by a white cloud as it opened up over the mountain; it was visible to all.

Soon the ship-cloud from the Mesa in Arizona appeared over Mount Shasta and the souls of the bound finally went home through that vortex. Mount Shasta is a place of ascension, know this; many come to ascend. The Indian tribes know this is the place.

The town was abuzz. "What were you doing on the mountain?" They asked us as we walked back into town. "We could see the vortex open-it was you, we know!"

We've never told the story to anyone but Charlie when we got back, until now. This is spiritual living-living on the battery terminals; negative and positive currents pulse here daily. It is the greatest challenge and the greatest blessing at the same time.

If you are ready to become a more enlightened being and take up this challenge to raise your soul's light, we may begin.

Thank you, Charlie Red Hawk Thom;

Many never even knew you, even though they stood in front of you; yet many others saw the Spirit that always was present within you, your love and compassion to all.

I am thankful that I know you.

May your words of wisdom still speak across the Earth.

A Word to The Casual Traveler It is not necessary that you come to Mt Shasta to go on a mission quest or have a great vision if you do not desire it.

Simply by coming here you will find a rest for your soul from escaping the city, noise and traffic jams! That in and of itself, is reason enough to come. You will have the opportunity to rebalance yourself with the sights and sounds of nature at its finest!

All around Mt Shasta you will find opportunities for good food, fun and relaxation!

Listed at the back of this booklet you will find the locations to many of our sights and activities. It's a great place to bring your family, go skiing or sledding at the Ski Park on route 89, or have fun camping!

In Mt Shasta City you will find the KOA Campground. Don't miss the Siskiyou Lake Campground; it comes with a spectacular view and beautiful lake for swimming on hot summer days! You may want to camp on Mt Shasta at one of the State Campgrounds. Panther Meadow, Bunny Flat and McBride Springs are favorites.

But remember, you are on sacred ground; respect and teach your children to do also. You will be blessed!

CHAPTER 6
ENLIGHTENMENT & MOUNTAIN MIRACLES

Pilgrims at Mount Shasta Upper Parking Lot in Ceremony

Not blurry; it's ENERGY!

We stopped the car to take that above picture with our cell phone camera. The entire mountain was glowing with a mist that was in motion, reaching up to the heavens.

It was surreal; fascinated, we watched.

How? How can a mountain do that?

We watched as the mountain decrease its glow before we got back in the car. How beautiful! Frightening? Not at all.

This mountain glows with a holy light and with purpose.

The Night is Calling;

I remember the first time I stood on Mt Shasta. It was at 2:00 am. I had driven straight to Mt Shasta and headed up to the mountain after my plane had landed in San Francisco. I had driven directly up to Mt Shasta because it had called me in dreams from my home in New Hampshire. I had been compelled but I did not quite understand why. I had received my call; but I did not understand the meaning.

The mountain itself was glowing in a soft blue light that night in November of 1999.Stars shown so brightly on the mountain snows, it felt as if it was nearly daylight! I will never forget it. I knew then that one day I would have to return to live here. Four years later, I would come to live at Mt Shasta in fulfillment.

So many travelers have spoken to me of The Calling. They too have been summoned in dreams and visions to make this sacred pilgrimage. Perhaps that is why you are reading this booklet and would like to have some assistance. Nighttime on the mountain is magical. Stars too!!!!

Can you see her? Mount Shasta reveals ancient legends and stories in many ways. Here she shows us the era of an age long past in the snow. Once, gentle Native Women packed their children, blankets and walked the deep snows.

Mount Shasta remembers; she draws her memories in the snows. So many people miss this blessing. They rush up the mountain with eyes that are completely closed. SLOW DOWN!

There are unseen guides. Here a woman walks her child. Native

Americans lived and died at this mountain; Shasta does remember. Nature records every thought and deed. The rocks are crystal recorders and the freshly fallen snow forms the images.

If only to have eyes to see...

Mount Shasta honors her little creatures that live in the woods too! In the softly falling snows, she fashions their shapes in the deep snow. This big squirrel seems to be enjoying some favorite snack!

A Mountain Miracle

One afternoon in late July, 2007 we had gone up the mountain to mourn the loss of our wonderful dog, Misun. You already know what an incredible, faithful dog he was! Our hearts were broken.

Misun had died suddenly and we'd had no chance to prepare ourselves.

We sat weeping while a snow cloud formed over the peak of Mt Shasta. The snow blew around us as we remained in the car and watched the unusual snow fall. It seemed as though the mountain was purifying us from our grief

After a few minutes the snow stopped and we looked up at the mountain's peak and were astonished!

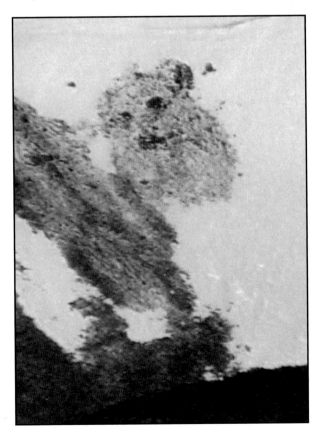

"How could that be?" We wondered, amazed and awed at the

sight before us! Our tears of sadness were instantly turned into tears of absolute JOY! The freshly fallen snow had formed an image!

BUT it was a thousand foot image of our dog in between the peaks of Shasta and Shastina!

Not only was there the image our Misun, but also another image of the little bear cub that had died from its injuries. Earlier that year a car that had hit the little cub.

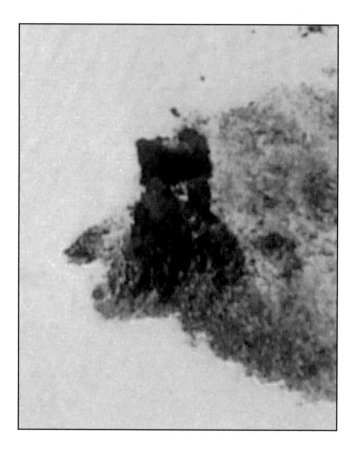

That truly is the Love of God made manifest at a very sacred mountain! People that I have shown these pictures to have cried tears of relief. Many of us have lost our beloved best friends, our pets. Their hearts were broken at the thought that they may never see them again.

Please, let your hearts be comforted in the knowing, the proof before you now, that your pet lives on, even as we shall, in the heart and mind of the Creator. Nothing is ever lost in the Mind of the Creator! I know we will see all our furry friends and companions again!

Just think how we have such a loving God! Imagine that! He can perform this miracle for just two human beings with broken hearts, over a dog.

Imagine what He shall do when this world is over, our training on earth is complete, and we enter the new creation! This is just a school, remember that.

It is no wonder that people come here to this mountain to heal their hearts! Creator is very close here, but always with us everywhere.

While you are here, take time to release your pain and loss to the mountain and to Creator God that hears all our prayers.

Mountains across the earth have been known to be places that we may connect to our Creator once again. Before the following chapters, I ask you to open your minds and to further consider the unknown.

I would like to say here that we have many languages and cultures to understand and respect. In our world, names and words many have many meanings.

The same words or names, spoken in another language are sometimes shaken off as 'inconsequential', or not Biblical, but may contain bits of truth pertaining to your own belief system- if you rise above your own beliefs, and can hear them.

Thinking in this manner causes division; we ought to be seeking bridges to understanding through respect for one another and for other cultures. At least think before you act.

If the European and Spanish had stopped for a moment they may have discovered the Native culture had many wonderful gifts to offer and truths to teach them before slaughtering so many, thinking that the Native was somehow inferior.

Again, the "I want" mentality and the "elevation of self" over others beliefs and customs had destroyed so much without even an opportunity for examination or explanation. What a terrible loss!

Indigenous tribes and cultures have centuries of knowledge of the earth, plants and spiritual knowledge we ought to be seeking.

All cultures have something to offer us if we can hear it.

Found in the area above Castle Lake, this ancient one could tell us many tales.
I am sure.

In the following chapters, I am going to relate personal experiences using names or terms you may or may not have heard before. If they are unfamiliar to you, please hear the messages contained.

Hidden blessings abound at Mount Shasta!
Even when clouds are dark, the blessing of rain comes to provide new life!

CHAPTER 7

LOOK CLOSELY

St Germaine in the air with an angel of Light.
1999 Susan Isabelle

Look Closely Now

The above picture was taken in 1999 while I was at the McCloud
Lower Falls.

In the center you will see an image of a man with golden hair. He is wearing a monk's brown robe and he is reaching up to an angel of light in the trees. He is hovering about thirty feet above the river beneath him.

This is St Germaine.

He has been seen by many others on or around the mountain. I'd had my first experience with St Germaine in 1997. He suddenly appeared to me and gave me instructions as to how to do earth healing and to teach the earth healing to people in classes. I saw him again in 1999 at Shasta.

This picture was taken near what I now call, "Kuan Yin's Temple."

I first moved to McCloud in 2004 because of this experience I'd had in 1999 on my first visit to Mt Shasta. The energy here was like no other place I had ever traveled to previously. I could feel the air!

I ought to mention here that I do not 'channel'. Spirit has shown me that to *embody* another entity within me, to bring forth their messages, causes us to lose our own being because of the merging of two.

The merging of two into one causes a loss of *our own soul's unique personality or integrity*. I only believe in merging with my Creator. That power of life is given to us when we ask for this merging; it is a very special gift from Creator. I "listen" instead. I do hear-a lot!

In 2004 I camped out in the Fowler Campground for the summer just to re- experience this energy. I was not disappointed.

One afternoon a friend from out east had come to visit me. I told her about St Germaine's presence being here, showed her the picture, and told her how much I loved this place.

But on this day in 2004, I walked with her down by the lower falls of the campground. We sat by the flowing waters on a rock.

Suddenly, the air began to sparkle around us and I heard a voice speak to me.

> *"I am Kuan Yin; this is my Temple*
> *and I wish to speak to Caroline."*

"Caroline!" I gasped! "Kuan Yin is here! This is her Temple and she wants to tell you something!"

© Goddess Kuan Yin by Susan Isabelle

The Jewel Is In The Lotus

Over the next few minutes, I spoke the words I heard from the sparkling air around me to Caroline, and then it all subsided. We sat for many minutes assimilating the information.

I heard Caroline's "OOOOH!" beside me. "Susan look!" she exclaimed.

Across from where we were sitting, the stones by the waterfall seemed to be moving, extending themselves outward toward us. Soon we could see a form. I share this picture I took with you now. It is untouched. This is the actual picture of that day that I very excitedly took.

Kuan Yin's Temple Lower Falls McCloud

I've outlined Kuan Yin's stone statue for you. It may still be

75

seen but is most often more recessed into the stone wall. In devotion, it will rise up for you to see also.

We watched as little pink flowers started to blossom at her shoulder and at her feet. We cried with joy and complete awe as this Divine Aspect of Mercy and Compassion had revealed herself so profoundly to us.

When you go here you will see children playing, jumping into the pristine waters, fishermen and tourists wandering about serenely.

People will be taking photographs of the statue and the waterfalls without even knowing that it is there or what it is.

Now you know what this place actually is and the power of its true spiritual nature. Kuan Yin is known to about a third of the world's population; maybe more, but is unknown to the vast United States' peoples. We need her message!

Here in California, we have a temple dedicated from the ancient past, probably from the times of Lemuria, to Kuan Yin, The Goddess of Mercy and Compassion! Its' right here in our own back yard!

I ought to mention that there's a lot more on this stone face wall. During the day the shadows form images of eagles, Kachinas, ancient Egyptian figures and sentinels.

Look closely and you can see the Sun Goddess Kachina in the photograph!

The Divine Feminine, the female side of Creator, has aspects or characteristics of her personality that manifest to different cultures. All one, but in differing names and forms to meet the needs of the individual culture. The Divine Feminine manifests to each culture such as Mary Mother of Peace, Kuan Yin, Mercy and Compassion, and IxChel, Protector of Children, and Shekinah, the Wife of God.

Remember, Mt Shasta is also "Shastina." As such, she has a feminine aspect within its own formation. We would do well spiritually to understand this about the sacred mountain energies we all seek. It would be difficult to ignore the spiritual energy that flows out from this mountain in its manifest feminine aspect.

Balance in the world and within us may be found here by tapping into the energies that flow even beneath our feet.

There are meridians of spiritual currents that move outward from this mountain that connect to all areas of the globe. Tibet is nearly opposite Mt Shasta, going through the earth.

At the Shambhala Center in the middle of town, you may actually experience one of these flows. Simply ask and you will be shown where it is and how you may come into balance. Glastonbury has the only other spot like this that I have personally experienced. Some members of The Rosecrucians came once to check it out. They believe this particular line is an extension of the Rose line.

I understand what Charlie, the Karuk Elder and my friend meant about his interpretation of a balanced personality. He called this mountain the 'battery terminals!' Your battery has negative and positive, male and female polarity, and so does this mountain.

You may have heard it expressed this way; if one has too much yin, the yang will arise. Too much yang? The Yin arises.

If one has too much aggressiveness, the mountain will bring you down into the arms of your own need of compassion. It will teach you through experience.

If one is too meek, one will be required to attain strength. It's all about the balance of male and female, the negative and positive aspects of even ourselves.

Our western culture has forgotten much of the teachings of the aspects of the Divine Feminine and as such our culture has suffered greatly.

The imbalance that has been produced has led us into corruption, lack of mercy, compassion, lack of love and respect for one another, intolerance and greed.

Now we, society, are creating our own 'solution'; we reap the works of our own imbalances. Now, we will need mercy, we will need money, we will need love. We will be brought back into balance one way or another. The Universe has laws too.

Scripture teaches us that the presence of the Holy Spirit, Shekhina brings love, joy, peace, understanding, and hospitality.

Use your time here to self- examine your inner balances and use the energy of the mountain to restore your balance.

It is much less painful that we each find the balance individually rather than society suffer destruction and the subsequent restoration needed to bring us back into balance.

I believe a sacred pilgrimage ought to be done by every human being at least once a year to restore balance. It is that important to come back into spiritual attunement with Creator and Nature.

Where are your feet taking you?
What path do you walk?
Can others follow you? Do they want to?
Do you need to change?

Walk this mountain to find your answers

CHAPTER 8   MEDITATION

A Sacred Feminine "Shekhina," Meditation

Inviting the Presence of the Holy Spirit, Shekhina

1. Find a place outdoors where you can connect to Mother Earth. Kick off those shoes! Connect with Mother Earth!

2. This is best done on a Friday evening. If you can, travel up Mt Shasta to the highest parking lot that overlooks the city.

3. Make sure that you light a candle to (MOTHER) or Shekinah, the Wife of God. Honor her for the sacred birthing of All of Creation and the Christ.

4. Ask for the presence of the Shekinah-Mother to surround you. She dwells in the very highest realms of Creation and shares the Light of the Creator in all Love.

Divine Mother is first movement of Love and consciousness before form. She is expressed through the emotion of Love.

That pure love takes on physical form as Earth Manifestation of the 3rd dimensional realm we exist within and are a part of. All you can see is of 'Mother.' We enter her womb.

She lives to bring forth the design and purpose of the Father-Creator Dream as an act of Love. In this, we are her children *when we bare the likeness* of that design. We with our free will can *remove ourselves* from the wholeness of this balance.

She has promised to be with Her Children as a guide and protector. We need her more than ever now that humanity has removed itself so far from this purity of Light and has lost its design of perfection. Shekhina! Most Beautiful!

5. Honoring her, reach up with your left hand. You will feel her touch your hand with her Light.

This Light is her Presence; God Consciousness, God awareness-and we need it! Shekhina, Mother wants to love Her child!

6. Breathe her in through your crown, drawing your hand downward toward your crown chakra; breathe in love and

enlightenment of the Feminine Aspects of Peace, Love, Joy. Compassion, a newness and Completion of Self.

7. Fill your being with Purity; not 'white light'! Not any guide or master! Only be filled the Light that Created YOU!

In the Mind of the Creator, you are perfection! Become one with your Creator and the One that loves you! Restore your DNA to the true template of you, not anyone else!

8. Ask to be reconnected with your true being, let Mother recreate you in her womb of love! and the true template of you-without any imperfections at all!

9. Let this flow inside, dispelling the old; filling you with the finest Love!

10. Breathe out releasing the lower aspects of yourself while saying or expressing,

"My mind is reconnected to the Mind of My Creator. May I see as they see and understand as they know..."

11. Reaching up again and asking Divine Mother for her love,

Breathe her in through your crown, drawing your hand downward toward your throat chakra;

"May I speak words of Beauty and kindness, of Creative Power and of this Purity to all mankind."

Contemplate your previous actions and release on your breath.

12. Reaching up again and asking Divine Mother for her love,

Breathe Her Presence in through your crown, drawing your hand downward toward your thymus (HEART) chakra;

"Mother, I ask that my heart be filled with the love that only you can express; the love for and of one another, of all creatures great and small, of the earth and of the entire universe, myself as an expression of your love in the world;

I am a reflection of the Thought of the Creator Divine, may I secure this within my heart and radiate this love throughout the earth."

83

Contemplate your previous actions and release those lower energies out on your breath.

13. Reaching up again and asking Divine Mother for her love,

Breathe her in through your crown, drawing your hand and the Presence within downward past the upper chakras toward your stomach chakra, stating;

"My mind and my heart are reconnected to you Mother, Father, Creator of All.

Now I release my will to your perfection. Let my life be lived according to your Divine Plan and will for my life"

Contemplate your previous controlling, destructive actions and release those lower energies out on your breath.

14. Reaching up again and asking Divine Mother for her love,

Breathe Her Presence in through your crown, drawing your hand downward toward your navel chakra;

"Mother, Father, by your power and strength, I ask you fill me with your incredible strength and power.

Secure it in my soul's earth connection, my hara, fully merging us as One restoring my total balance on the earth in accordance

with the plan and purpose of my life!

I release old ways of falsely connecting myself to others, places, possessions and things and fully embrace my True Power!"

Contemplate your previous actions and release those lower energies out on your breath.

15. Reaching up again and asking Divine Mother for her love,

Breathe Her Presence in through your crown, drawing your hand downward toward your root chakra, filling your entire channel with Divine Presence;

"Fill me Creator, with your Presence and secure your Presence through my root chakra and into my earth star to connect us to the earth always. Please remain with me always, guiding and protecting me, your child. For now I hold the image of my Creator, filled with your likeness and love. Now, we are One!"

Breathe out sending the Presence through your legs and securing all to your earth star. Christians! Remember!" Pillars of fire beneath my feet, I will walk in the house of the Lord forever!"

The Native Americans say that when we are filled like this we "bless the earth with each step we take."

16. Remain quiet. Contemplate the holy, sacred merging and love your Divine Mother and Creator of All.

Realize that when we are not in alignment with the Creator and this Presence, that we separate ourselves from the Divine. There are 16 spokes to the sweat lodge; the center opens to the Creator. The 16 spokes hold our physical reality and the soul's presence connection to Creator and Spirit is our channel to Light.

We lose our "Oneness" by the acts of our own will.

Our lives become chaotic and dysfunctional because we are not in balance, we can't find our way because we cannot see our own circumstances. Our 'impurities' prevent us. We've been contaminated by the world and its illusions.

When we view from the heights of heaven, we see and understand all. When we join the Light of Father/Mother within us, in a true honoring balance, something wonderful happens to us-the Creation of a New Being occurs; this is the acceptance of the Christ, the Only Begotten, first born.

The negative, positive, Father- Mother spark results and creates anew the Light, but within us-true meaning of the Christ within. Christ, the Son was first, we are subsequently made in that likeness. Scripture puts it that we 'die daily' meaning this is something to do every day to release the old way and embrace the new likeness of our true blueprint.

We literally become a new creation, the spark generated by the joining within us is the Light of Christ. "Christ in you, the hope of glory!" I quote the scriptures .Our DNA is forever changed.

When you do this meditation, you rejoin; you are One and nothing is denied you. Allow these moments of sacred bliss to bring peace and promise of a new you, a new life – birth, and a new balance upon the earth.

Relax in the knowing that you are loved, you will be guided

and your life fulfilled in its entirety.

Go in peace; avoid any outside worldly stresses or contact for at least 24 hours if you can. It has been my experience working with thousands of students, that those who do not take the time to do this correctly or honoring of the great gift they've been given, quickly fall back into their old ways.

A 'rebirthing' through the Divine Mother's Womb. The release of our pre-conceived notions of how things ought to be is required. Her perfect likeness is required within us, we take on-Light Up- the DNA of our true parents. This is how to activate it. DNA is transferred through the mother. The old worldly likeness must be released to receive the new form. It is being offered to you now.

You wanted change, didn't you?

Honor Mother, Father, Creator of All daily;

you will not regret it!

On this day we saw Shambhala… Dec 2004 a golden mountain appeared over the mountain's summit as we prayed.

The dimensions opened and we could see…Forever, Shambhala!

DNA/Bloodline of the Holy Grail

I have been conflicted as to whether or not reveal what has been brought to light to me recently. I have been seeking knowledge as to what I should do or not do. It concerns DNA.

Someone came into the store the other day and brought it right to me; "You have to write about the DNA, it's important you do that!" Without any previous knowledge about my discomfort about this DNA revelation, he said it directly to me.

I take that as a word from Spirit. Now, I must tell you, even though it may put me at some future risk. I honor those of all religions and beliefs because I believe all have a portion of the truth contained within. It is our task to compile that information without prejudice. But, this prophecy concerns all of us and specifically the Hebrew faith, and impacts all of us.

A great secret is coming to light;

Some of us believe that Christ took a wife and had children. All indications are that this is a truth. A Rabbi was expected to be married. Not to have children was considered a curse. Christ was not cursed, so it stands to reason that he did have children.

People point to Mary Madeline to be his wife but there is a much better candidate for that position in scripture that I will write about at a later time.

It is my personal belief that Mary Madeline actually went to France to care for the Blood of Christ Skull and lived in a cave. Her chapel exists to this day in France. (I wrote about this in the fourth book *In The Eye Of The Goddess.)*

The other Mary with her children or pregnant, traveled into England with Uncle Joseph of Aremathia and became what is called The Holy Grail. She is the grail, the Holy Cup that brought forth the new bloodline. I found her resting place also.

For nearly two thousand years her grail has overflowed with a multitude of children, grandchildren, intermixing DNA with others, into Spain, France and much of Europe and so forth across the earth. The gene strand of the Hebrew peoples was kept by restricted marriage within the same faith, that is until they were persecuted; they gave away their children to protect them, further mixing the genes.

Wicked Hitler sought to completely wipe out that purest form of the bloodline in the 1930's, nearly two thousand years later. It is now called the bloodline of the Ashkenazi and has a specific DNA code of N1b1.

This bloodline is traced back to one or two women first emerging in the area of Jerusalem at the time of Christ! Could that be Mother Mary and her offspring, her children? Or the wife of Christ bearing children?

Nearly 6 million Ashkenazi Jews of this purest strand were nearly exterminated during WW2, but persecution has been from the time of Christ. As soon as this 'light gene' emerged the war was on! King Herod was so afraid of it that he had all the children killed at the time of Christ's birth.

Many of those that survived the various periods of persecution fled across the earth hiding their heritage and intermarrying. The Spanish Inquisition during the 1400's caused these children to be given to protestant families. Into Canada and South America the people fled persecution. Some intermarried with native tribal women.

This seeding of the bloodline has continued from the time of Christ, and has been preserved throughout time. This previously has been thought of as the Jewish race but by now…

*Most likely nearly all of us have some of this Christ 'sown'
DNA within. With this, we have a choice.*

Christ spoke of this in more than one of his parables. We
couldn't understand it at the time because we didn't understand
DNA. We now do understand. Turn on the Light.

The most quoted example of this is in the parable of the wheat
and the tares; the farmer went into the field to sow his seed, then
the wicked came and sowed its seed in the same field. That's
DNA seed people. Realize is that this coming of the good seed
had to happen;

*The earth has been created in order to hold a specific race ;
NOT a race of color but a <u>genetic code</u>. It is that of those
made in the image of God, the Children of Light. These
children are those of mercy, compassion, great abilities and
balanced within their hearts and minds.*

The Anunnaki, a biblical race of fallen angels, or a hybrid race
had come to earth and mixed the DNA of the Creator's with their
own fallen race. They did this knowing full well it was wrong.

They did it so to order to control the population and make it their
own, the 'enemy's' seed. ***Their character is greed, control and
a heartless society that seeks its own agenda without any
concern for human suffering.*** (read Zecharia Sitchin's work
with the Summerian tablets)

We are experiencing their control right now. They have not gone
away and have tried to manipulate our DNA to this very
moment in time.

Many reading this today bear the DNA of *both* but the true Light
of Christ " grafts us into the family" if we, the gentiles, and even
those not of the original seed, desire it.

I believe they are attempting extermination even as we speak through chem-trails, 'fake snow' 'plagues', earth weather control and so many other means.

We are fed fluoride in our water and toothpaste, which blocks our code by crystalizing the pineal gland. WHY? The pineal gland gives us SPIRITUAL VISION.It is also the 'gateway' for the Light of Heaven to illuminate our true souls. With that vision and enlightenment,we can 'see' the manipulation and the agenda.

Many Christians fear the 'mark' which may be another attempt using a nano technology implant to permanently alter our genetic code to that of their own sick agenda.

At Christ's coming 2,000 years ago, he restored the DNA to the original blueprint. All this time it has been spreading and overcoming the darkness DNA of the fallen race. WE ARE WAKING UP! They don't like that one bit. Reincarnation has brought each camp many opportunities to change their ways.

Children of the Light now fill the entire earth.

The wheat and the tares have grown together across two thousand years. The time of harvesting is soon upon us, the tares will be removed and the wheat taken in and preserved. (Raptured)

Our entire earth is groaning beneath their crazy desire for money, power and control at no matter what the cost is to humanity. Our food, water, health and joy has been taken from all of humanity. We can only watch as the poisons they manufacture fill us with their cancers, but not for much longer.

I have fulfilled the prophecy of the 13th Crystal Skulls; the cry has gone out to heaven that we are ready to become as little children and that our hearts are made ready for a new creation.

We have been heard. We are not ignorant of these things. God has not left us without instruction or abandoned us.

I will write to you about the coming blood moons and the sign in the heavens in the following pages to help you understand.

All this is true and given to us so that we may understand the times and the seasons. I believe a last attempt is coming to exterminate the Christ DNA from the earth. The ANUNNAKI are coming to claim what they believe, and will enforce with horrific methods, are their own earth rights. Believe it or not, this is all about the claiming of title and having control. They never give up.

IT SHALL NOT SUCCEED. The Creator of All will restore this planet and the DNA of his own and that of his wife Shekhina, the Dove of Peace. Know that you never die; all will be restored.

In the meantime we have grown to fully understand the consequences of living under the rule of the enemy's seed and structure. I certainly don't want it anymore. I look forward to the day when all of earth is cleansed and a balanced, righteous, compassionate to humanity, love order is upon the earth.

Many of you reading this were with me on 7/26/2013 when I made you understand that the system we suffer under must be cleansed of unrighteousness. I called out to you,

"Do you know what we ask? Are you sure you want this?"

Hundreds of you shouted, "Yes!"

We proceeded to ask God to create the Rainbow Bridge with the Heart of the Child to bring us to a New Creation of Righteousness and Peace. We had a miracle and proof! Rainbows were brilliant in the sky that day over the Shambhala Center and all of Mt Shasta! A prophecy was fulfilled that day.

Only that change of our hearts will allow all of us to live in peace and harmony with God and nature.

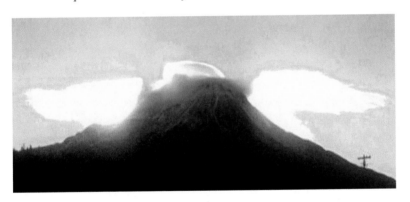

PHOTO OF THE DAY, SUBMITTED BY D. DICKSON TO MT SHASTA
NEWSPAPERS- CLOUDS SURROUND THE MOUNTAIN SUNDAY FEB.
2014 FROM BIG SPRINGS ROAD NEAR LAKE SHASTINA. "MT.
SHASTA WAS PRAYING FOR SNOW," DICKSON WRITES IN HER
EMAILED SUBMISSION. "SO BEAUTIFUL, THE SUN WAS JUST
COMING UP ON MY WAY TO WORK AND MT. SHASTA HAD A HALO
AND WINGS. I HAVE LIVED HERE FOR ALMOST 60 YEARS AND
HAVE NEVER SEEN HER SO BEAUTIFUL."
THIS WENT VIRAL ON THE WEB AND FACEBOOK
THANK YOU DD FOR SHARING! THE PEOPLE NEED TO SEE THIS!

CHAPTER 9

ARRIVAL TIPS

Arriving in Mt Shasta; A Few Tips

When you first arrive in Mt Shasta, you will need to dust off the city. Cleansing oneself to receive Divine messages or Presence requires we prepare ourselves.

People come looking for the Lemurians at Mt Shasta.
Some actually see them. I have on several occasions along with my students, in the Shambhala Center and on the mountain.
I know that they are very real.

They have an ability to manifest in physical, human form when the environment is correct. By 'correct', I mean matching the environment of that which they come from and live within. They are like the angels. It is possible to raise our vibration to allow them to come to us.

As they are higher dimensional beings, they do not exist within the mountain, but in the higher dimensions that surround this place.

So, don't be disappointed that you cannot drill a hole into the ground to find them, but rather, you must find the entrance to them through your heart.

And it stands to reason that if you are filled with envy, greed, hostility and anger, you will not see a Lemurian.

If you are polluted with entities, negative thought forms, and the presence of other entities are inside of you, you will not have a *real* spiritual experience here either.

People have taken to guided meditations and visualizations coming from their own minds to create a spiritual experience for themselves or to describe their spiritual experiences.

Imagination is a powerful motivation, but hardly what the true seeker wants from the spiritual realms.

You that are reading this booklet; you're looking for your own experiences and you want them to be real, tangible and life changing.

You want to know that there is a Creator and that you are loved. Imagination doesn't cut it.

Those of you that have had multiple meditative experiences and have brought into your channel " white light"; I have a sad message for you.

I wrote about this in some of my other books. ANYTHING that is not in a physical form is a 'white light' in the universe.

Yup- even Uncle Harry who is hanging out in the 4th dimension waiting to reincarnate because of past misdeeds, is just waiting for the opportunity to enter a body to speak for a while. Your body will do just fine!

So, if you have brought in white light, that must also be cleansed from you.

What can you do? You just got here at Mt Shasta and have picked up this booklet and now realize you've got a bit of work to do to get ready.

Here are some suggestions.

Upon arrival

1. Cleanse your hotel room.

You don't know who or what has been in there previously. We have room sprays that we distribute through Mt Shasta Sacred Mountain Herbals in our store at the Shambhala Center.

They are specifically developed to cleanse out unwanted thought form entities by using age old herbal remedies.

If you don't understand this, have you ever walked into a room after someone has had an argument?

You can feel the tension in the room. That lingers and collects over time. No place that you can visit can ever cleanse that emotional energy from your hotel room.

And then you wonder why you feel awful in the morning when you wake up. You're supposed to feel great on your vacation!

During the night your subconscious picks up all the energies that are around you. Are you upset or angry for no reason? Just what or who has your subconscious attached to?

We do know how to take care of that by using special herbs that nature has created for this very purpose.

FYI:

Smudging is not allowed in some hotels and believe it or not, smudging is a three part process. To be effective it requires all three steps to fully cleanse an area. So, just using a smudge stick does not fully cleanse an area.

2. Cleanse yourself.

Run a cleansing bath to detoxify your body's system. It will make your experience so much more enjoyable if you don't have to forcefully detox by the assimilation of powerful energies here. This is the gentle way. If your hotel has a sauna, make use of it! The sweat will allow you to release much more quickly.

Use a formula that contains Dead Sea salts, Himalayan salt or Epsom salt. All else failing, use plain table salt. Add this to your bath.

Again, Mt Shasta Sacred Mountain Herbals has prepared the bath salts especially for you and this for this very purpose. You may purchase them in town.

If time allows, you may want to schedule a detox bath at Stewart Mineral Springs in the nearby town of Weed prior to doing any serious energy work. The combination of the mineral bath and the sauna sweat works wonders!

3. After you complete your detox,

Spend some time in quiet meditation; determine what it is that you really want in your life. The Creator is ever close, especially in the energy of this sacred mountain.

Write out in a material form what you want to manifest in this lifetime. Take the thought and bring it into form...

4. Drink plenty of fluids

The mountain's elevation causes a fast dehydration of your body fluids. Make sure you carry water with you everywhere you go and drink it!

Energy workers will tell you that to do energy work one must consume double their normal amount of water and fluids.

Many people make the mistake of consuming alcohol and partying when they arrive.

Intoxicants further dehydrate your body and allow the lower energies to thrive as you are not fully in control.

To attain spiritual heights, the mastery of mind, body and soul is necessary. I can tell you that that does not happen when one is intoxicated with alcohol, nicotine, weed, mushrooms or anything else you might try. You are being fooled.

These 'mind expanding' drugs don't make the genuine connection to the Divine but to lower energies. You'll get a high but it is a false high, they open a doorway but not to where you really want to go.

Lower energies don't deliver anything but later misery and take the light that is within you.

5. Continue your spiritual practice

People always wonder why others have experiences and they don't. Those that do have real experiences with the Divine find that fasting, prayer, dedication and resolve to find the answers at no matter the personal cost, are the key.

You want to see Lemuria? You must be as a Lemurian.
Their lives are pure and gentle, they laugh and play as little
children in total innocence.

Once I had a group that had lifted their light so high in our classes, I had so much fun with them- it was wonderful!

We all joyfully went to the Upper Falls in McCloud. We wanted to experience the energy of Lemuria.

As we were nearing the big waterfall, an elderly couple materialized on the path in front of us. Dancing and skipping as children they past us and simply disappeared!

We laughed and continued on our way as if it was the most perfectly natural thing! In this energy, it is.

6. Make a sacred journey

Go up onto the mountain or to one of the sacred spots at the mountain.

Find your sacred space and create an altar. It can be of pine cones, pine needles stones or crystals you have purchased and cleansed previously.

Remember to respect the area and in the Native way, leave no indication that you were ever there. Clean up!

7. Start out by doing the Reconnection and Rebalancing Meditation as previously described.

Once the mountain recognizes your purity and connection, it will open up the doors to you and welcome you into the Sacred Mysteries.

The world comes alive as Spirit is now free to bless you, teach you, and to guide you!

Let the magic of Mt Shasta begin!

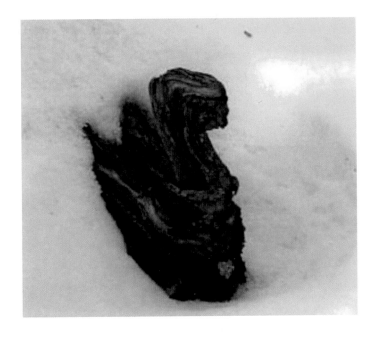

See that little green heart on the swan in the snow?

That's a message on a little branch.

The swan represents the Divine Feminine.

Her little green heart is telling us of her love and healing...open your eyes! It's all around you!

Chapter 10   UFO'S and Angels

Speaking of things that be all around us...

Of course, you'll want to know about the UFOs that are here...actually, everywhere.

Our Star Brothers and Sisters visit Mount Shasta pretty regularly. I've had several encounters and write about my dinner with an alien in my first book, "On Assignment With Adama." He was a beautiful soul.

But, you want to know about Mount Shasta. Will you see one? Once I was at the upper parking lot one night with about thirty others. We had completed drumming and dancing a sacred spiral. Yes, I just gave you a hint about how to build the energy to see one.

All stood still as I brought the Sacred Heart,13th Crystal Skull

Heart, to touch each participant's heart. As I stood in front of each person I would take the two skull's pieces and bring it together in front of the person. This symbolizes the coming together of the male / female minds to form One Heart, One Mind in alignment with the Creator of All.

*Note. OK. You don't have a skull- but anytime you demonstrate this 'sacred coming together' on the mountain, you honor the energy of Shasta-Shastina and begin to build the energy. You may want to get two 13th Skull activated crystal skulls from us and just watch what happens!

Just as I was performing this in front of a woman, she began screaming! "They're coming together! They're coming together!"

Thinking that she was referring to the skull, I tried to reassure her. "That it's OK- they are supposed to come together, that's how the skulls are made."

Wide eyed, she anxiously pointed upward behind me. I turned to see two big saucer UFO's speeding toward one another. They were coming together.

As this was happening, four other 'stars' seemed to rearrange themselves into a big square shape. The two UFO's were speeding toward the center of that square formation.

All of us were watching the heavenly spectacle. "Are they going to crash into one another?" We wondered, holding our breath.

They neared ' crash point', but suddenly veered at the last millisecond and flew upward into the center of the Star Square Portal way and disappeared!

It was as if the UFO's were demonstrating to us the 'Coming Together" and ascension! Do they watch and listen? Oh, yes.

They have fun too! Some are really nice!

What I am telling you, teaching you, is that sacred balance of Mother/Father is required for ascension and for creation. Even the star brothers and sisters know that. It must begin within each of us, that rebalancing and acknowledgment of these very spiritual teachings of Mount Shasta and Shambhala, Heaven's Light.

Another story...

Many months later my partner, Jeremiah, and I were sitting up at Bunny Flat on the mountain in our car. It was now the middle of winter and the snow was piled high. There were several other cars there also. We were facing down the mountain.

I don't even remember why we had decided to go up there that night; the road was snow covered and dangerous, but we had come just as the others had.

It was about midnight or a little afterwards that we were discussing the earlier UFO coming together event that summer.

"Jeremiah, I've seen lots of small UFO's; eleven at one time in Mexico were hovering over us, but I've never seen a UFO up close." I said.

No sooner had the words come out of my mouth when Jeremiah

said, "Well, look at that one!"   We watched a UFO that looked like the mother of all mother ships glide right over the road in front and above us.

It was absolutely silent, was glowing, and must have been about the size of the City of Mt Shasta!

I have no more desire to see one up close anymore. I think those that were there with us that night don't either, but I think we were "called" to see that event.

Also, on the night of New Year's Day, 2014 we went up the mountain well after dark. 'Called' once again we watched five orange colored UFO's dance across the sky over Northern California and Oregon. Many had called in to report the sightings to the police and local stations.

For some reason, they want us to know they are watching over us. I find it comforting- as long as they don't declare to be our 'creators,' I'm OK. Yes, there are also negative Et's out there too.

In the next 3 years there are going to be many things happening. Spiritual Travelers! You are going to be needed. I will share some prophecy with you now. It is more than prophecy, it is fact. There are going to be signs in the heavens. You may well want to be in Mount Shasta or another sacred mountain area during these times.

Let me explain.

As I write this I am reminded that one year I went up the Mount Shasta to the upper parking lot on Rosh Hashanah with a group to pray at sundown.

It is the time of opening the books of life, and a holy day of those of the Hebrew faith.

As we prepared to sing as the sun began to descend, we waited and watched as three robed persons came and sat on the ground beside us.

They started to sing before we did. It was so beautiful we could not even open our mouths! When all was done, my group, softly crying, walked away. I went to the three to speak to them. When I approached, their hoods dropped down. I stood in the presence of three angels all with massive black and golden locks of hair.

I couldn't speak, but they did and told me they had never met, or to do this on this mountain before- they had come from different places from across the earth to do so.

Barely able to speak, I thanked them and humbly departed. When I turned around to look back, they had disappeared.

Some of you reading this will remember.

"Calling All Angels!" REMEMBER!!!

Does Mount Shasta have to do with the Hebrew nation and prophecy? Apparently so, as these angels had come to worship God in song on that holy day with us. And with me, holding the Sacred Heart Crystal Skull!

Many of you know that I study prophecy from around the world, that I look carefully into current events and also to the scriptures of the Maya, Sumerians and the Biblical prophets.

Chapter 11 Prophecy 2020
What I have discovered must be shared!
Hanukkah meaning in <u>Hebrew</u>: חֲנֻכָּה or חנוכה
English translation: "Establishing" or "Dedication"

Let me begin; on the 1st day of Hanukah Nov. 27 [th] 2013, a Hebrew Holy Day, the Menorah (eight candles) of Hanukah was 'lit' in a spectacular way. It was 'established in the heavens.' Below is a Menorah. The center candle is lit on day one. It just so happened that a heavenly sign was taking place at the same time.

The first candle, the Center Candle of the Menorah, was lit by **Comet ISON (I-Son)** on its perihelion, the point when it was closest to the sun. It was not by chance that this happened. It lit up as a great flame. Most never understood the significance of the comet's arrival on that day as it swung around behind the sun.   The first 'candle' lights all the others.

It started with a <u>Heavenly SIGN</u> so 8 <u>Heavenly SIGNS</u> will follow. Travelers listen. A Heavenly Lighting of the Center Menorah Candle, happened right on Hanukah! The menorah reminds us of the miracle of the Hanukkah lights, when only one day's oil burned for <u>eight days</u> after the Maccabees reclaimed the Holy Temple. It was the beginning, the first indication about something and I got really curious.

I-SON. A coincidence? Was Christ lighting this? Was this an announcement? If you know me, this is a challenge and a CLUE! I had to start researching. If this was an announcement from heaven, then I wanted the message in full. If the message STARTED in the heavens, then it was also logical that the FULL MESSAGE would come in heaven. It would most likely also have to do with the Hebrew nations.

I found in study that after the center candle is lit,
8 more remain, one to be lit each "day".
Now, instead of days, consider that it represents a month, a year,
or an undetermined period of time, Or Events.
Example; 8 years =8 candle, or =8 events.
To follow the pattern being set in heaven; there are 8 more
candles in the Menorah. Logically, that means there are to be
more "8 signs in the sun, moon and stars." There are.
I believe something big is going to happen.

So researching I found that what I was feeling was in fact true! Check this out; there are coming more heavenly events!

I found that 6 of those signs were on their way, and
VERY SOON!

6 more heavenly signs fall on Jewish Holy Days within a 2 year period. We need to pay attention .What does this really mean?

It means that there are 6 identifiable markers in time, set in the heavens to tell us something;....wow... read 2nd chapter of Acts and 21stst chapter of Luke!

BUT, there was even MORE! I learned about a tetrad, a rare heavenly series of signs and what they mean.

2014 - 2015 Jewish Holiday Eclipse Schedule

15 Apr 2014	08 Oct 2014	20 Mar 2015	04 Apr 2015	13 Sep 2015	28 Sep 2015
Jewish Passover	Feast of Tabernacle	Jewish New Year	Jewish Passover	Feast of Trumpets	Feast of Tabernacle

The Blood Moon Tetrads & Eclipses of 2014-2015
April 15, 2014 Passover -BM
October 8 2014 Feast Of Tabernacles- BM protection
March 20, 2015 New Year- FULL Eclipse of the Sun
April 04, 2015 Passover-BM
Sept 13, 2015 Feast of Trumpets-Full Eclipse of the Moon
Sept 28, 2015 feast of Tabernacles- BM

A **blood moon tetrad** is when 4 total lunar eclipses occur (consecutively) on a Holy Feast day. Because of the angle there is a reddish tone to the moon.

This will not happen again for one thousand years!

Every single BMT has brought a significant event to the Jewish people within a year of the first or last eclipse of the tetrad.

The first tetrad occurred in 1492 during the Spanish Inquisition. Jewish people were forced out of Spain with a two week notice or death. They gave away their children to protect them as they fled the country. Also, Christopher Columbus found the New World that would later become the safe haven for every culture and tongue fleeing persecution. *Persecution-then freedom.*

Then the next tetrad was in 1949-1950. At that time, in 1948 Israel became a state again and the Israeli war armistice was in 1949. 6 million Jewish people were *exterminated, then freedom.*

In 1967-1968 there was another tetrad. During that time Israel came under attack and through many miracles Jerusalem was captured by Israel in 1967. This was during the 6-day war. These are extremely important events in Biblical prophecy and eschatology. *War then freedom* for Jerusalem, the Holy City.

Now, do you see the pattern developing?
We are in a tetrad. So, if this holds to form we may expect a time of Troubles; then, Freedom
(There is another; a hidden sign which may come in May or October 2014 It may be another comet. That would make 8 total)

I believe these signs will produce a consecutive series of world altering events that will lead up to the 7[th or the 8th] sign.
It is a spectacular sign
The Sign appears in the heavens on Sept 23rd, 2017

A WOMAN CLOTHED WITH THE SUN,
She has
THE MOON BENEATH HER FEET,
WITH
TWELVE STARS IN HER CROWN

It is the Virgin Queen; Virgo. At this very moment in time, the constellation Leo appears over the constellation of Virgo, the Woman. This forms the 12 stars of prophecy in her crown. Look, there are 12 stars.
Pictures are from various sources available internet and astrological source

What is it? Study Revelation 12: 1&2
The moon is at her feet. The sun is clothing her..
She is about to give birth as Jupiter (The King) is birthing.

This was also seen at Christ's birth. It is the star that the Magi followed. They knew that Jupiter in this position meant that the King-Son was coming!
It means the SAME THING AGAIN!
Christ is returning.
This is His sign in the heavens.
If my studies are correct, then this date is the
7 year MID_POINT SIGN.

Those of us that have followed Biblical Prophecy know the mid-point of the last 7 years would have a spectacular sign in the heavens. We must prepare and pray. Because there are 3 1/2more years to go.

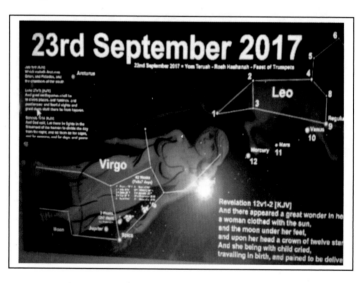

It means that after this sign appears, I believe all the Candles are lit; we've seen the SIGNs come and go and this is the final phase. We need to pray fervently.

Remember that I didn't put it in the heavens, God did. In the Book of Daniel, prophecy was given by to him by angel Gabriel, and Jesus gave confirmation of a future event, a covenant "with many" will be made for a "final week" -7 years. I believe we are at that point.

Finally, the Return and Justice will prevail, the Lamb will lie down with the Lion. It will be over in 2020-21. A New Creation is coming. I am excited!

Pointing out the October 2014 Feast Sign; another comet is coming that is expected to engulf Mars. It is the Feast of Tabernacles.

Perhaps the 'hidden sign' is around Rosh Hashanah A time for rapture? Weikipedia states,
"In the Talmud tractate on Rosh Hashanah, it states that three books of account are opened on Rosh Hashanah, wherein the fate of the wicked, the righteous, and those of an intermediate class are recorded. The names of the righteous are immediately inscribed in the book of life, and they are sealed "to live."

The intermediate class are allowed a respite of ten days, until Yom Kippur, to reflect, repent and become righteous; the wicked are "blotted out of the book of the living forever."

"No man knoweth the hour" Jesus said about his return to take up the believers and church. There is a clue for us regarding this particular feast day and heavenly sign. "Sealed to live."

Will this be the time of a rapture? Possibly. We wait and see. We are told not to set dates because no one really knows. Is this date a good candidate? I think so, but there are also a few others that shine.

I realize that some of you do not understand what the Rapture is. Many believers know that Christ will come in the air to take up the believers in The Creator of All, the Holy Spirit and in the sacrificial work Christ did at his first coming.

Those that believe in the sacrifice of His blood and the forgiveness of sins and have asked for that forgiveness, that call upon His Name to be saved, shall be freed from the final judgment. They will be 'Raptured' just before the final judgments. That series of judgments is of the fallen angels and of those that remain on earth. It is their final opportunity to ask for forgiveness. Then the end of the rule of the fallen angels and extra- terrestrials will come. Christ returns to set up a Kingdom on Earth that will last for a thousand years.

There will be peace, joy and prosperity for all. There will be no darkness or a 'dark side' you of self you must try to accept. That will be completely done away with. No more fallen angels will be around trying to prevent humanity from attaining their fullness. We shall finally be freed from their influence and control.

Are you of the belief that you are God? That as God you'd never sacrifice your own son? Well, dear friends, what you have been taught will have to be reconsidered. When the events begin to happen, you will have no other option than to consider what you have read here. Christ is mercy and truth. You may enter when you ask.

Many of you reading this book have followed my work since I started my Spiritual Traveler assignments. Do you remember what happened in Machu Picchu?

Machu Picchu Peru; 11-11-11 The Sign Of The New Birth. See the baby rising up as the Peruvian looks on?

11-11-2011 The Promised New Baby was in the sky. The government was there along with the United Nations. We kept getting in the way of their taking pictures. A BIG Birth Announcement was in the sky when we opened the way! At the Mid-Point Sign that birth is shown in the heavens. Now is the time; 9/23/2017 for the event. Jupiter, representing the King is birthing at the feet of the woman. Christ, the King is coming soon!

Christ will not come as a baby this time;
the birth is of a new world.

Machu Picchu was also a Sign; 11-11-11 the doorway was opened with the Sacred Heart. The New Creation is about to be birthed. The Second Coming and a whole new earth recreated by the Son of God is coming.

And it's not going to be an extra-terrestrial claiming to be our creator. They are going to try that one, the fallen angels. Don't you believe it for a moment!

For 15 years I have been following the directives from Heaven and have seen many miracles of healing, miracles in the sky, the waters and the earth. I have seen the Greatness of the Creator and I believe.

The Sacred Heart, in the crystallized, manifest form is to remind us, to prepare us. The 13th Crystal Skull was given to the Maya to hold until the end and the new beginning. They knew they had to give back their own hearts to God one day. That's why it's a child's heart.

Just as we celebrate communion in our churches in remembrance of Christ, the Maya had the 13th Skull to remember they would one day give back a sacrifice- one of their own personal heart- to God. It would be at the end of time. I have been given the responsibility of taking care of that 'stoney heart'.

We must become as little children to enter the Kingdom of Heaven, Shambhala, the Golden Age, and the Kali Yuga. All are signals of a new world! Not a 'new world order' Travelers!

It was also a sign to humanity that it is time to return our hearts and our minds to the Creator of All. Christ is the physical, human, Sacred Heart. There is also a prophecy that on the last day, the 'stoney heart' will be returned to Him. I can't wait to give the heart of stone, the 13th crystal skull back to Him! Then we receive the New Heart, and a new way of living. It will be balanced.

We have held the hope and the promise of a new template all across the Earth with the Crystal Skulls' abilities. The coming years will require that we all know prophecy, the use of the Name, and the Fire Codes.

The Name; remember those that call upon the Name shall be saved! The Name of Christ, "SHIN" is in the codes. USE them and call upon the Christ!

I have fulfilled prophecy regarding the skulls. The skulls have already 'have come together' as many of you wait; it wasn't in a little room. The skulls were designed to 'come together' across the ENTIRE EARTH!

It happened on top of Mt Shasta in 2007 with 24 countries participating! All across the earth the message of the skulls was pronounced. We came together! 'IT IS DONE!" We all heard it at the same time; the Name of God was sent around the world as prophesied, "When My Name is heard throughout the earth, then shall the end come."

God said it and we did it with the Light of God, His Name and the skulls of consciousness that were placed to establish the global Name. We now look forward to the new coming Creation and Christ. Now it is time to prepare and come into understanding;

I have believed that Israel's becoming a nation (1948) again marked the last generation (70 years) that Jesus spoke of that "shall not pass until all these things have happened," before his second coming. I was born in 1949 and have known this would come in my lifetime.

So, when does the final 7 years BEGIN? Using the 360 day Hebrew lunar calendar specified by 1260 days, we count backwards from 9/23/17 the mid point of the final 7 years to find the *beginning*. The date of April 13th,2014 is the result.

I now believe 4/13/2014 marks the actual beginning of the 7 year event; Palm Sunday, just before Passover, 2014, the 1st Blood Moon Tetrad

Additionally, Jan 11, 2014 just as I was writing this book, Israel's Ariel Sharon died after having been in a coma for many years. There was a specific prophecy regarding him and his death.

What is important about this in prophecy is that it was declared by a very respected 108 year old Rabbi Kaduri (who claimed he had a visit from the Messiah) that the Messiah told him he would come after Ariel died.

This Rabbi shocked the people of Israel because he declared the Name of the Messiah to be Yeshua, Jesus the Christ.

I encourage you to go to the youtube.com channel and look up *The Art of the Covenant found, Blood Moons, and Bible Codes* to see the wonderful work of others that are also seeing the same things I am in the sky, on the earth and in scripture.

Then think about these things for a while. When I was sixteen I came across an old postcard from the 1930's that was in a wall in my first apartment.

On the postcard I read, *"Be thou faithful until death and I will give you a crown of life." Jesus*.

Raised only with my catechism from the nuns, I had never seen ANY scripture, Bible or prophecy until that very moment. It went into my soul and began my search for God and the meaning of this postcard.

Susan Isabelle

We are here Spiritual Travelers

This is the moment of Truth; All shall come into truth in the
Light-But remember this
Absolute Truth is only in the Mind of the Creator of All
As Light increases within, be flexible; for what you thought was
true today may come into change tomorrow with
Fullness of the Light
Seek wisdom
No matter the outcry against Christians ,against Christ, or your
belief in the Creator of All-
All will be challenged in the days ahead- across all nations and
tongues, lineages ,beliefs, and cultural practice
Purify your hearts and minds
Forgive
the sins of pastors, priests, congregations, parents
the bad experiences you may have had with fellow parishioners;
friends or family members, yourselves

The Name is above all; Call upon the Name
Pray
The signs are in the sky.
Stand tall, hold your Light and don't let anyone take that
from you. We never die, only transform into Light
Seek peace and harmony with all mankind as you are able
Prepare yourself.
The change is here; challenges will arise; have faith
Celebrate Passover this year; celebrate each of the Feasts.

Now you understand
BELIEVE

I think I'll go up the mountain.

Perhaps you'll join me here at Mt Shasta at the Feast Days Maybe the angels will be there again. We'll sing together.

Chapter 12   Places to visit while at Mt Shasta
For a Sacred Pilgrimage start out at Castle Lake

Mt. Shasta Area Campgrounds - Mt. Shasta Ranger Station, Mt. Shasta CA (530)926-4511 voice, (530)926-4512 TTY-TDD

Castle Lake Campground - From Mt. Shasta City, head west on Lake Street over the freeway and to the stop sign at Old Stage Road. Turn left (south) and drive ¼ mile to a fork in the road. Stay to the right at the fork and continue on this road, W.A. Barr Road. In 2 miles you will cross the dam at Lake Siskiyou and then you will see the turnoff for Castle Lake. Turn left and drive the paved road 7 miles to the lake. Castle Lake Campground is located ¼ mile below the lake on the left (east) side of the road.

One spring I awoke to gentle, angelic voice, "Go up to Castle Lake today."

I arose thinking I must have been dreaming, looked out the window at the piles of snow.

"This can't be," I thought, "I'd never make it up there." I went into my store, then located in Weed, and some travelers came in.

"Can you tell us where Castle Lake is?" They asked the question of the day.

"Yes, follow me; I got a message to go there this morning from an angel, so I guess we're supposed to go together."

The young couple was delighted! "I do have to tell you that the road is likely to be snowy-you may need chains.".

"That's OK, we're ready."

We made the trip up the road as far as we could go. The road was closed off from the snow.

"We'll have to hike the rest of the way, but it's not far."

As we walked, I told them the story of the early settlers encountering the Indians who told them not to go to the lake-there was a 'demon spirit' there, so they said.

"I don't believe that for a moment." I told them. "Every time I have come here I have only felt the welcoming Spirit of the Divine Feminine, and She's beautiful!"

We trudged through the deep snow until we were close to the area of the lake.

121

"Before we enter here there is something you must do." I instructed. "Stop right over there, at those two trees and ASK permission to enter this sacred space. Follow me and do as I do!"

Once all of us had made it through the gateway to the lake, we struggled through the deep snow. "WHY?" I thought, "did Spirit want me to do this today?"

Then I looked up across the lake- we all did.

"OOOOH.. MY GOD! WOULD YOU LOOK AT THAT!" We all exclaimed. On the other side of the lake was a vision so beautiful! It confirmed to the three of us what I had just been saying earlier...this is the place of the Woman Of The Lake!

Before us in the snow was a huge 'portrait' drawn on the cliff face across the lake, perfectly made of snow.

A great angel was standing with a sword touching the top of the head of a woman. She had long white hair that was made of locks of snow.

Her bodice clearly seen, formed by the rocks beneath outlined with snowy detail, her dress extended down into the lake where the swirled snow had formed her dress!

I cried, we all cried. What a blessing! The Angel was anointing this vision.

From that time forth I have brought homage to Her, brought students and have asked for her blessing of Spirit.

I was given a song here too.

Prayer of the Waters

"Spirit waters, sacred waters,

flowing to the sea;

coming home to me,

Spirit waters, sacred waters,

purify my soul,

cleanse and make me whole…

Spirit waters, sacred waters

coming home to me,

Setting the people free

So when you go to this lake, go and ASK to enter this holy, sacred ground filled with flowing waters of sacredness. Her waters are alive, sacred, purifying and cleansing. They are a flow from the Spirit ,a living consciousness.

Dip seven times and release your old energy, prepare for the new. Cleanse your soul. It is a baptism.

We all share the water of the earth, a cloud here- rains some other place across the globe. Someday we all share this same precious spirit of water.

Sing to the waters, tell her you love her, tell the next person partaking of the same fluid to heal with the sacred waters now available to all .

How we have abused the consciousness of this planet. It's message is human polluted, but we can change that.

That consciousness is held within her waters, within the earth, sky air and sea, within you and me.

Now, pray for all to be free. Susan Isabelle

I wasn't able to get a picture that day…who would have known, but I did take this one of a cloud formation later. It is a woman looking down over the lake…

Going up Mount Shasta.

I am always surprised that our travelers do not realize that you can DRIVE up the mountain! The primary access road for Mt. Shasta is the Everett Memorial Highway

Lake Street is the central exit for Mt. Shasta City (Exit 738). From Interstate 5, take Lake Street east (toward the mountain). You will drive through the business district right past the Shambhala Center in Mt. Shasta City before the road climbs a hill and changes names to Everett Memorial Highway, also signed as county road A-10.

The Everett Memorial Highway ascends the south side of the mountain, starting at 3500 feet in town and terminating at timberline near 8,000 feet.

The local Ranger Station and visitor information is located in the town of Mt. Shasta at 204 West Alma Street.

Access to the mountain is open and free to the public at all times. Be aware that the facilities on the mountain are limited. There is no piped water available, so be sure to bring some with you. Toilets and information boards are located at Bunny Flat, McBride Springs campground, and Panther Meadows .All other services are found in the town of Mt. Shasta.

Panther Meadows located near timberline on Mt. Shasta at 7500 feet it is the highest campground on the mountain with open views and vistas.

Mount Shasta City Park

1315 Nixon Road, Mount Shasta, CA 96067
The Headwaters of the Sacramento River are hereLake Siskiyou
Camping, swimming at Mount Shasta, CA 96067

Fowler Campground and McCloud Falls

RT 89 5 miles east from McCloud intersection

Hedge Creek Falls

4121 Dunsmuir Ave, Dunsmuir, CA

You can walk down to the falls and sing, pray and experience the energies here, then go to the beautiful botanical gardens a short distance away.

Strong elemental energies are there. Go play with the water fairies and gnomes! In the botanical gardens, if you sit quietly and ask, you may have a little one sit near you. They are quite friendly here.

Medicine Lake is located about 30 miles Northeast of Mt. Shasta

The lake sits in the caldera of an ancient volcano called Medicine Lake Volcano. The most recent eruptions took place about 1,000 years ago on the east side of the rim (called Glass Mountain).

The elevation is an amazing 6,700 feet, and the lake covers nearly 600 acres. Medicine Lake has special spiritual significance for local Indian tribes, who frequently use the lake for ceremonies.

Lava Beds National Monument

From the National Park Service Website:

"Over the last half-million years, volcanic eruptions on the Medicine Lake shield volcano have created a rugged landscape dotted with diverse volcanic features. More than 700 caves, Native American rock art sites, historic battlefields and campsites, and a

high desert wilderness experience await you!"

The Monument is also a site of historical significance: it was the site of one of the last Indian wars in the west.

The Modoc Indians held off the US Calvary for months until they were finally captured. There are a number of historical markers in the area that allow visitors to follow the battles.

The Monument also has hundreds of caves. Many are open for exploration.

Other resources

For more details about mountain camping sites visit
http://www.fs.usda.gov/detail/stnf/recreation/?cid=stelprdb5134255

**The Sacred Heart, 13th Crystal Skull of the Maya at
Mount Shasta may be seen by appointment at our store**

Call the Shambhala Center   530.926.1331

101 West Lake St Mt Shasta City 96067

email   susan.isabelle@live.com

website;   www.crystal-skulls-mayan.com

Also; www.MtShastaHerbals.com

For herbal preparations made in Sacred Mount Shasta

Susan Isabelle's Books on Amazon.com and at the Shambhala Store

On Assignment With Adama

The Global Assignment, The Cosmic Eve 2012

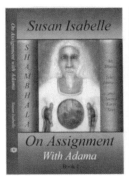  

In The Eye Of The Goddess, Return the Goddess,

Truths And Deception of Higher Self Teachings

The Spiritual Traveler's Guide To Sacred Mount Shasta Prophecy 2014-2020

Messages From The Heart Of Great Spirit

ABOUT THE AUTHOR

Susan Isabelle has been a resident of the Mount Shasta area for nearly ten years. She is of the Native Iroquois tribal lineage(Roy) originating from Quebec, Canada. In 1999 Susan came to Mount Shasta because of a dream she'd had that called her to the mountain. At Shasta, she met the Lemurians, her life changed and was sent on a mission- quest by them that has lasted for fourteen years!

She became Keeper of the 13th Crystal Skull in 2004. The Maya gave it to her in Belize while on a Lemurian mission. She was instructed by the Maya to learn how to use the skull to assist humanity.

Susan relocated to Mt Shasta to fulfill prophecy at the start of the Venus Transit June 2004. There she offered the 13th Skull, the Heart of the Child, back to the Creator to fulfill the Maya and Christian prophecy.

Her Lemurian Earth Mission ended 12/21/2012 at the end of the old 26,000 year dream of Creator, but Susan has continued on to help at the beginning of the establishment of Creator's New Dream. On Mount Shasta with hundreds of students and friends, 7/26/13 she ushered in the Year of the Galactic Seed to fulfill prophecy of the Christ Light's Creation Return to request of God that promised new world that is coming to humanity.

She continues the work at her Shambhala Center in Mt Shasta and across the entire earth!

Made in the USA
Middletown, DE
23 August 2021

46789876R00077